GunDigest® BOOK OF

SURVIVAL

GUNS

Tools & Tactics
for Disaster Preparedness

SCOTT W. WAGNER

Published by

Gun Digest® Books, an imprint of F+W Media, Inc.
Krause Publications • 700 East State Street • Iola, WI 54990-0001
715-445-2214 • 888-457-2873
www.krausebooks.com

To order books or other products call toll-free 1-800-258-0929
or visit us online at www.gundigeststore.com

Cover photography by Kris Kandler

ISBN-13: 978-1-4402-3384-5
ISBN-10: 1-4402-3384-5

Edited by Jennifer L.S. Pearsall
Cover Design by Dave Hauser
Designed by Rachael Wolter

Printed in the United States of America

ABOUT THE AUTHOR

Scott W. Wagner

is a law enforcement veteran of 32 years. Currently a sergeant with the Village of Baltimore, Ohio, Police Department, he previously spent 20 years with the Union County, Ohio, Sheriff's Office as a reserve deputy, where he worked patrol, training, and S.W.A.T. and was the Assistant S.W.A.T. Team Leader and one of the sniper teams. Prior to that, he worked as a full-time patrol officer for eight years at the City of Reynoldsburg, Ohio, Police Department, including two years as an undercover narcotics officer at the regional Metropolitan Enforcement Group in Licking County, Ohio, and one year as an undercover investigator for the Ohio Department of Liquor Control. Wagner has been a state certified police firearms, fitness, and defensive tactics instructor for 26 years and has been a criminal justice professor and police academy commander for 20 years at a community college in the Midwest. He is the author of the Gun Digest books *Own the Night—A Guide to Tactical Lights and Laser Sights* and *Tactical Shotguns*.

DEDICATION

No work such as this would be possible without the support of family and friends. I wish to thank my wife, Bobbie, for patiently putting up with me and two gun safes in the house, including one in the bedroom. I also wish to thank my sister-in-law, Mandy Hughes, for her photographic work and contributions. Several of my police academy cadets participated as models in the photos, and I appreciate their efforts, as well. Many thanks to the Special Forces operators, who provided their insight, as well as my law enforcement friends, who have suddenly realized the seriousness of this topic. Finally, thanks to my friend and survival expert "Bill," who helped confirm my concepts were on the right track. I also wish to thank the following manufacturers and companies for providing test and evaluation materials for use in this book:

Bates and Dittus

BLACKHAWK!

Century International Arms

Crimson Trace

Del-Ton Firearms

DPMS

IO Firearms, Inc.

Food Insurance

Ithaca Firearms

Lasermax

Marlin Firearms

Maxpedition

Maglite

Mossberg Firearms

For those of you who have chosen to be ready, and who may have suffered some ridicule for your beliefs, I would offer this. There was once a man named Noah. He prepared an ark to save his family and the animals specified by God from an impending flood that God said would wipe out all animal life from the earth. It took Noah and his family many years to complete this work. Although the Bible does not record it, there is no doubt that he was the object of ridicule and scorn by those who were soon to be wiped out. Keep preparing. While we hope the things we are preparing for never come, we want to be ready in case we do. We owe that to ourselves, our families, and our trusted friends.

CONTENTS

INTRODUCTION

A ccording to the National Geographic television show *Doomsday Preppers*, approximately 45 percent of the population has been preparing at various levels to cope with some form of upcoming societal upheaval, either at a local or national level. The forms of calamity that motivate individual "preppers," as they are called, are myriad, ranging from comet strikes and volcanic eruptions in Yellowstone National Park to localized disasters such as tornados and hurricanes, and on up to things on a national or even global scale, such as would happen in a complete economic collapse. No matter the reason for the crisis, the concepts for survival are the same: provide for long-term food, water, medical supplies, and the general security needs for yourselves, friends, and family members, when the traditional needs of substance provision are either temporarily or permanently unavailable. While there are a number of survival guides both from FEMA and private sources available to the public that promise to cover this topic, there is very often one aspect overlooked, and that is the selection of weapons and tools that provides the best security for prepared families at a reasonable cost.

Gun Digest's Guide to Survival Guns covers not only the selection of firearms, but other concepts such as layered defenses, caliber selection, action types, ammo types, carry methods, and commonality with other weapons systems. An examination of support gear, including carry and storage systems, along with transport modes and deployment (Chapter 12, "Emergency Evacuation: Needs Beyond the Gun"), is presented and contrasted to weapons systems and defense methods already in place for those potentialities. Pre-disaster travel will also be explored, as well as a discussion of triggering events. Recommended firearms training plans are also scrutinized.

The *Gun Digest Book of Survival Guns* should appeal to a wide variety of people interested in long-term survival, whether the endangering event is on a local, state, or national level. Cops, civilians, and soldiers—everyone who is interested in keeping themselves and their families intact when these perilous events occur—will find useful information in this text, regardless their stage of preparation or belief system. An intense focus on practical firearms to obtain prior to these events sets the *Gun Digest Guide to Survival Guns* apart from other works written towards this topic. I hope you will find this information and the concepts presented therein helpful.—*Scott W. Wagner*

A well-stocked survival food supply. This is essential where you're planning on bunkering down for the long term, a concept known as "sheltering in place."

Chapter 1

WHAT'S THE BIG EMERGENCY? WHAT'S EVERYONE WORRIED ABOUT?

It is clear there is a deep-running fear throughout a large portion of the United States population, one at a level unseen since the Cuban Missile Crisis days of the Cold War in the early 1960s, when I grew up. Although I don't remember actual "duck and cover" drills, which I think were phased out as being rather useless at the end of the 1950s, I do remember the crisis and people building personal bomb shelters. I remember that, while my dad didn't build us a bomb shelter, we did have extra food stored in the basement for an emergency (though I'm not sure it would have been enough for our family of four). I also remember the myriad buildings designated as official Civil Defence fallout shelters that were stocked with food for the supposed long-term survival of as many people as was possible to fit inside.

This Civil Defence emblem could be seen posted on many buildings in the 1950s and '60s, identifying these places as bomb shelters.

Fortunately the bombs never fell, and the specter of nuclear war grew faint over time. But, while the concept of some form of preparedness waned, it never disappeared. When it came back, in 1992, it was due to the election of Bill Clinton as President, and this time the preparation carried with it a major focus on obtaining and stockpiling firearms and ammunition, particularly because of the 1994 Assault Weapons Ban; the concept of food storage and the reinforcement of the home didn't seem to be as much a part of that. The people who loaded up on guns were only in part thinking of armed resistance against the government, and an even smaller portion of that populace gave thought to what such a resistance might entail. Most of the other people were thinking about buying and hiding the guns they acquired—that's when the backyard burial and storage vaults first appeared.

What was also a part of the '90s preparedness movement was the appearance of unofficial militias for defense against government intrusion, a response against the perceived threat of "big" government. So not only did folks individually prepare, some also joined groups (or at least until they were turned off by some of the radical thoughts harbored by some of them). And while the election of Barack Obama as President fueled an even bigger rush to buy guns and ammo—Obama is often referred to as the largest gun salesman in the history of the U.S., with Bill Clinton running a close second—there are new underpinnings to twenty-first century preparations. While there is still concern over government interference, it seems to me that the major concern is now our fellow citizens, those who will be motivated to rob, kill, and steal in order to survive due to a major societal and economic collapse of the type that is already starting to affect European nations staggering under a huge burden of unsecured debt. Or, worse yet, debt secured by Communist (yes, I said Communist)

China. (You know, the same folks that send us poisoned dog food, lead-painted kids toys, and who slide counterfeit, defective, electronic parts for aircraft and our weapons systems through the military procurement channels.)

There are some other issues playing into our current situations. I think the fanatical obsession with "zombies" in movies, books, video games, and on television is indicative of this shift in fear from government conspiracy theories to the fear of masses of people as our main threat. However, in this fantasy fear world, dangerous people are given the form of zombies, who can't be reasoned with or talked to, who aren't deterred by less lethal means, and who only succumb to the deadliest of force. Ironically, this is actually the way real mobs may respond when the desperation level is high enough. The entire zombie "explosion" has become more than mindless entertainment. The "zombie apocalypse," as bizarre as it sounds, has become code for many who are preparing for their version of impending mass social disorder.

I'm no psychologist, but it may be that saying something weird like, "Ah, I'm just preparing for the zombie apocalypse" to someone who asks why one has so many guns and supplies deflects the seriousness of the topic by treating it as if it were a big joke. In this way, the person who gives that answer isn't seen as a whack job who thinks his fellow humans are going to be a huge personal threat someday. This doesn't mean the person who gives such a flippant answer actually *believes* the people attacking them will be true-life zombies. It just means they don't want to divulge their true feelings to others, appearing, instead, to be playing a game. Further, it is possible that engaging in this type of mind game is a way of building in some sort of operant conditioning. Perhaps so strongly associating the fictional creatures with masses of starving (not for brains) human beings in the midst of a real emergency builds an association that serves as a way to dehumanize those people in advance and prioritize the defense of one's self and family.

This zombie obsession has spread to the point that it has reached, or should I say "infected," the firearms and related industries, which now market zombie guns and ammunition. There are also zombie knives and other edged weapons, as well as specialized zombie targets and shooting competitions. While some of this is simply gross fun, it has proven even more popular than the recent vampire and werewolf craze. There has never been a vampire or werewolf shooting craze out there, perhaps because the fictional zombie can be felled by conventional ammo applied to the brain. Werewolves can also be killed by firearms, but only if the cartridges are loaded with silver bullets. You are mostly out of luck on vampires as far as shooting them goes, at least according to legend. But maybe there's actually more to this phenomenon.

I am sure a very real part of the zombie fascination is evidence of our overall cultural decline. Look at the difference between the modern zombie, vampire, or werewolf movies and the original Frankenstein or Dracula films in terms of the graphic gore displayed. Heck I watched the most recent Wolfman movie and had to shut it off due to the huge amount of gore (and don't tell me I can't handle gore, as to date I've done 32 years as a cop). Compound movie gore with the graphic and brutal violence in modern video games, and we have an entire society that is being desensitized to death, torture, and mayhem. And *that*, folks, is in part what will make the public reaction to a twenty-first century economic collapse (which is what I personally fear, not volcanoes or comets), much different than the societal fears that began in 1929 and lasted until the start of World War II, in 1939.

In the event of collapse, everyone who is able will need to "provide for the common defense," male and female, young and old. Here, Azar, one of the author's students, is equipped with a long gun that fits her slender build perfectly. The Auto-Ordnance AOM-150 a splendid reproduction of the WWII M1A1 Paratrooper carbine. Weight, length of pull when open, semi-auto operation, and lack of recoil make it a perfect choice for her.

We have lost our historical moral fiber and with it our unity as one nation under God. Any talk of morality or faith in God in today's popular culture is held up to ridicule. During the time of the Great Depression, we were a moral nation united. We helped and trusted our neighbors and looked out for them if not personally, then through our churches and synagogues. There was no welfare system back then on the scale of the model we're familiar with today. There were relief payments from the federal government, but that was only meant to stave off starvation. Economic conditions were horrid, with 25 percent of the male working population out of a job (few women worked, in terms of having a career). Yet while liberal criminologists always blame poverty for crime, during the time of the Great Depression and its dismal conditions, crime was extremely low and isolated. My dad told me that, during those years, it was still safe to walk through Central Park in New York City at night. There were no school shootings or cops needed in schools, there were no incidents of a man eating the face off of other men (now *there's* a real example of a zombie!), or crazed individuals throwing their self-eviscerated intestines on police officers trying to help them get medical and mental health attention. There was none of the vulgarity and cruelty we see, hear of, or face today. Most churches were kept unlocked. Cemeteries were never desecrated. Rifles and shotguns could be shipped to your home via the U.S. Mail (and actually get there), as could handguns, until 1934. Hardware stores sold Thompson submachine guns for protection against cattle rustlers, and target shooting and hunting were honored pastimes. This is not the "gold old days" musings of a guy in his fifties, it's an analysis by a cop whose college coursework was in history.

We have been separated into nearly warring factions over issues of class, race, and religion. To further compound matters, large segments of the population have been raised expecting government handouts for nearly three generations now. This segment is not used to making it on their own, or even being motivated to do so. Too, in this same population are large numbers of illegal immigrants of various stripes and motivations, and contrary to popular belief, not all of them are here just to work on fulfilling their desire for the American Dream. Many are here as part of the drug cartels or other criminal or terrorist organizations and have no interest whatsoever in being a part of the great melting pot that is our American culture.

What are people like this going to do when the funding and checks

The author stands ready to defend his property, armed with a 1942 M1 Garand afixed with a bayonet. The Garand works great for sheltering in place and covering long-range threats, but a weight of around 11 pounds loaded and an operating system that spews its key components—the En-bloc loading clips—all over creation make it less than desirable for emergency evacuation strategies. If you're bugging out, think lighter and less conspicuous.

stop because the government can't print paper money that's worth anything? What will they do without the moral constraints that had been passed from generation to generation *en masse* in this country for the previous 200 or more years, even in schools, and not just in isolated pockets, as is seen today largely through home or private schooling? They will do just what a bizarre fortune in a fortune cookie my wife opened up one night said to do: "If you want it, take it." And, like the zombies on TV and movies, they won't care how they take it or whom they have to hurt in the process. Further, if it gets bad enough, what happens when the police and the military abandon their posts (as some 300 New Orleans cops did during Katrina), to take care of their own? And that is what will happen, especially if they are no longer getting paid to stay on duty. *You will be on your own*, (just like you actually are in many cases right now), defending yourself and family, and you need to ready, ready to defend them with deadly force when the moment requires it.

What is Civil Unrest?

Simply put, civil unrest can be defined as a widespread disruption of normal daily activities in a given geographical area. Disruptions include, but are not limited to, lack of protection and assistance by public safety forces (police, fire, and EMS); destabilized food and water supplies; interruption of electrical power and phone service (both land line and/or cellular service—remember that, during the 9/11 attacks, national cell phone service was down due to system overload, and only land lines worked); limited or no gasoline availability; compromised hospital care; and a host of other issues that may not be foreseeable. What separates civil unrest from the individual conditions that combine to define it is the feeling by a large number of people that the previous societal, personal, or moral restrictions that had been keeping themselves and the society around them orderly no longer apply. Thus, roving mobs or gangs of these "liberated" people are now roaming the streets intent on taking whatever they want from whomever they can get it from by any means necessary. There is no negotiation or pleading with such groups. If you do not have the ability to resist their predations, whatever you possessed previously, including your life and the lives of your family, will be gone in the aftermath of your encounter with them.

As I write this, it is the aftermath of the Colorado movie theatre massacre, and also the Sikh temple shooting, both committed by psychotics who were mentally functional enough to be extremely

There are so many modes of handgun carry available that there is no excuse for not carrying—this includes law enforcement officers, who should always carry when off-duty. The author is shown drawing a Beretta M9A1 from a Maxpedition Sitka pack's hidden compartment.

dangerous. With 12 dead at this time and 70 wounded, the Colorado movie theatre shooting stands as one of the largest number of casualties inflicted by an active shooter to date, and the way this nut job booby trapped his apartment, it was possible some first responders could have been killed or injured in the mitigation effort (fortunately, none were). This is just another in a long string of events that began during the Clinton administration, events that used to be almost non-existent. Now these events seem to be getting more and more severe, while the incidents that cause fewer casualties are too numerous to even keep track of.

Because of the Colorado theater incident and all the other active shootings, I have realized something. We already are in a period of civil disorder, although it is pre-collapse. We are in civil disorder because our moral underpinnings are gone. If you are a cop reading this and you don't carry an off-duty gun with you every day, and I mean *every* day and everywhere, then you need to hang up your badge and gun. (I personally wore down a lot of shoe leather walking the miles of legislative hallways in Washington, D.C., back in the 1990s, pushing for the right of all cops to carry firearms when off-duty and when later retired, anywhere in the U.S., through H.R. 218, The Peace Officer Safety Act). If only there had been one armed off-duty cop or legally armed citizen in that Colorado theater to take that psycho out, the casualties would have been far fewer.

We are in the midst of disorder now, and the only thing that hasn't happened to make this *uncontrollable* civil disorder is that there hasn't been a total governmental collapse. We are not yet living in terms of day-to-day survival. But it isn't far down the road if we continue on our current path.

When true civil disorder reigns supreme, you will have four major immediate needs that you must provide for:

Food, water, and medical supplies are your top priorities in a time of civil disorder, as are shelter and maintaining your physical safety. Just remember, stores like this are great if you're staying in one place, but if you can't quickly evacuate with it, you're going to have to leave it behind. Have a plan for both scenarios.

1. **Food and water.** Without these two things, anything else on this list becomes an exercise in futility.

2. **Shelter.** The incident may come during the winter or during other harsh weather conditions. In fact, it may have come about because of harsh weather, such as a tornado, hurricane, fire, or blizzard.

3. **Medical needs.** This is particularly important if you require prescription support medications for daily well-being. Back up until the time I turned 40 or so, the only support medications I needed

were a multi-vitamin, maybe some over-the-counter allergy pills, and an occasional Excedrin. At age 55, that is no longer true. Up until a few years ago, I loaded up the medications I needed in a pill minder, with only the amount needed for the days I would be gone. Now, with the thought of not getting back home as quickly as I might want, I travel with full pill bottles of my medications.

4. **Physical safety.** I mean this to include protection of yourself, your family and friends, and your supplies. The latter is the part groups like FEMA never mention in their preparation materials. The government as it is currently constituted, and this includes at the national, state, and local levels, will never recommend (with few exceptions) that you obtain a firearm for protection in disaster situations. That is what this book is all about, to complete the missing component from other disaster preparedness manuals and show how firearms blend in with the other items needed for short- and long-term survival.

The Police and Military Will be There, Right?

I've been a cop for 32 years. If I was called to duty in my nearby village of Baltimore, Ohio, and the unrest or disaster condition was widespread and affected my home area, well, I'm sorry Chief, but I'm staying home with my wife, particularly since she is totally blind. (In fact, I *did* stay home from my teaching job and with my wife during the release of the exotic wild animals from their cages by their mentally disturbed owner in nearby Zanesville. I loaded up my M1 Garand and kept an eye out.)

The first example I ever saw of a large number of cops abandoning their posts during disaster was during Hurricane Katrina.

The author stands ready to defend his wife, who is totally blind, and her guide dog, Charlize. His M1 is loaded with a full eight-shot magazine of FMJ .30-06 ammo in order to deal with any of the dangerous exotic animals released from the Zanesville, Ohio, compound after their mentally ill owner committed suicide, an incident that made national news headlines.

Upwards of 300 New Orleans PD officers left their posts, I assume, to assist their families. This widespread abandonment of post didn't happen anywhere else that I know of in the path of the Katrina—then again, the civil unrest and looting didn't occur anywhere else, either. It took cops coming in from all over the U.S. to stabilize New Orleans.

At first, I blamed the "blue flight" on the poor reputation of the New Orleans Police Department itself. But I realized later that this may not

In current conditions, police officers are available to assist you 24/7. If there is a major catastrophe that involves and endangers officers' families, the possibility exists that they may not be available to assist you. You will be on your own as far as defending yourself and your family, as police will be unavailable as they defend theirs.

have been the case, nor the only motivating factor. The officers that fled *may* have needed to safeguard their families in the face of the disorder; remember, their situation wasn't like that of the people who went to Louisiana to help but had no personal stake in the affected area. The New Orleans officers had their families right there at ground zero. I imagine that, had there been only the physical elements of the disaster to deal with, far fewer may have abandoned their duties.

But Katrina wasn't the only time there have been problems with police protection in the face of disaster. In any other time of civil unrest, police presence has been scattered and spotty, at least for the opening salvos of trouble. Eventually, public safety forces rallied and/or were joined by other departments or the military in mutual aid to stem the violence that was occurring. We now know that, when public safety departments are prepared well in advance, there is far less carnage and destruction. Note the difference between the first World Trade Center meeting in Seattle, when agencies weren't ready for anarchists, and any of the subsequent meetings. The worst situations that arise are those we aren't expecting—hence the saying "forewarned is forearmed."

The Rodney King post-trial verdict riots in L.A. are a perfect example of the damage that can ensue when public safety organizations aren't in a state of readiness. As this nation witnessed, the LAPD was clearly unprepared for what happened in the wake of the trial in Simi Valley in which the officers accused of beating King were acquitted. The violent reaction in South Central Los Angeles was beyond the ability of units on routine patrol at the time to handle. Combine that situation with an administration that was initially timid about taking necessary action, and you have a major civil unrest event. Fortunately, the unrest did not spread citywide, but the damage in South Central was massive, and many individual civilians (such as truck driver Reginald Denny, who inadvertently found himself in the middle of the violence, was pulled from his truck, and beaten to the point of brain damage), suffered in the backlash. No one was safe.

Multiple shops and stores were burned and looted during the chaos—*except* for the stores owned by Koreans. Those folks understood the real meaning behind the Second Amendment—much more so than many of the native-born proprietors. The Korean shop owners stood outside their stores or on their rooftops with rifles and shotguns and, amazingly enough, the crowds left them alone. The looters and

INSTRUCTIONS
Push button, and Public Safety Officers will respond immediately. Please use only in emergency cases.

GAI-TRONICS CORPORATION

HELP

If society as we know it collapses, kiosks like this will be of no use. Neither will the 9-1-1 operational system nor your cell phone.

rioters knew they would be shot where they stood if they attacked.

During the L.A. riots, not only were there no police available to stop the looting, there were also no police available to stop the looters from being shot! This brings up another point of order. The riots occurred in 1992. Even though it was before the Clinton Assault Weapon Ban of 1994, the AR-15 (and the AK-47 to some extent), held nowhere near the popularity as it does now. Colt's was still the only game in town then. Most of the photos I saw at the time showed the store owners armed with pump shotguns, lever- and bolt-action rifles, and assorted handguns. One video on YouTube shows a shopkeeper on the rooftop of his business with an over/under shotgun.

As you can see, if you don't have one of the current crop of high-cap magazine-fed guns available to you for whatever reason, all is not lost. No one in control of their faculties wants to get shot, so that lever-action .22 stoked with 15 rounds of high-velocity Long Rifle ammo may be quite enough to stave off a very large band of people intent on harming you. And while you're chewing on that, remember that the most important thing to take away from any of the media about the L.A. riots was that the police and National Guard were nowhere to be found.

Nothing has changed since then. You will be on your own.

What are *You* Prepared to do?

In the 1987 movie version of *The Untouchables*, Sean Connery's character, Officer Jimmy Malone, asks Kevin Costner's Elliot Ness, "What are you prepared to do?" Initially, Ness wasn't prepared to go to the extremes Officer Malone indicated would be needed to take Al Capone (Robert DeNiro) down. Later in the film, after trying the conventional way of obtaining evidence for an arrest, Ness, following

If you can't afford a semi-auto military-type rifle, or can't legally acquire one because of a ban, all is not lost. Marlin's 1894 C lever-action rifle holds nine rounds (one in the chamber, eight in the tubular magazine) of .357 Magnum ammunition, or 9+1 of .38 Special ammo. It can be fired rapidly and accurately. Recoil, even with full-power 158-grain .357 rounds, is very mild, with 110-grain +P+ .38 Special Winchester "Treasury Loads" milder still. The author backs the Marlin with a Model 67 .38 Special Combat Masterpiece equipped with Crimson Trace Laser Grips.

some soul searching, agrees to do it Malone's way and, in the end, after a great deal bloodshed, is able to take Capone down.

When we talk about disaster and disorder preparations at the level we are concerned about, there is also a lot of soul searching to be done. It is one thing to face an attacker armed with a knife or gun or other obviously deadly weapons, but what about a crowd armed with rocks, bricks, or makeshift clubs? What if the crowd is comprised of people of various ages, including women and children? What if they are totally unarmed?

When I conduct training in mob and riot control for law enforcement cadets, I emphasize that dealing with a crowd is the most dangerous activity there is in law enforcement. Crowds can turn from a group of quiet, curious people to mindless, deadly mobs in seconds, especially if you add alcohol. You can be torn literally limb from limb by an unarmed mob before you can finish the thought "What the … ?"

Based on this harsh reality, you have to ask yourself what you are prepared to do in the event that disorder suddenly enfolds around you. Compound that question by throwing in the variable of what if some of the mob members are your neighbors and maybe even previous friends. That really complicates things, doesn't it?

You may be looking at taking actions you never before contemplated, so the time to contemplate your response is *now*, not when the balloon goes up. Indeed, start thinking before you even read any further. While you are pondering that question of what you would do, try this one as well: Are you willing to break what had previously been the law before the calamity began? Now, officially, I am not advocating that you break any laws, especially now or perhaps in the near future when there may be a little semblance of visual law left. I'm just asking the question, because it will be a road that, if not needing to be crossed, will need to be contemplated.

All in the Family

You will be outnumbered in every outbreak of civil disorder. You, the law-abiding, peaceable, doesn't-bother-anyone-else type of person, will be in the minority. So, too, will be the cops, and anyone else who believes in a moral and orderly society. This dictates that you are

It is important to protect family members not capable of protecting themselves. The concepts here demonstrate that 360-degree protection is essential. You have a point man in the lead at the 12 o'clock position (shown with an IO AK-47 and military AK bayonet). At the three o'clock position is a member armed with a Century International Arms AKM with a folding metal stock. The team member at nine o'clock is armed with a vintage WWII M1 Carbine with bayonet, and at the six o'clock, the rear guard is prepared with the 9mm Century International Arms UC9 Carbine.

going to need "force multipliers" when it comes to defending yourself and your family. Force multipliers can be in the form of superior weapons and the hardening of your home, shelter, or vehicle, and/or the addition of increased number of able bodies, i.e., your family. This means your spouse or significant other, children, siblings, or parents will need to cowboy up and be ready. They need to be able to defend your stronghold, vehicle, themselves, and you. It will be impossible for you on your own to do it all and, if you become incapacitated, do you really want to leave your family to beg for whatever small piece of mercy might exist in that mob? The end result could be expected to be somewhat like our pioneering frontier ancestors experienced when their settlements were overrun by raiding Indians. Not a pleasant thought for anyone.

How able-bodied does your family need to be? How about this: can they hold a gun (of a size that fits them) and pull the trigger? Can they discern friend from foe? Can they pull the trigger when it is aimed at another dangerous human being—even if that dangerous human being was once a friend? Can they hit what they are pointing their gun at? If you can answer those questions with a resounding "Yes" for each person, you are good to go, and the "Yes" members receive equipment and training suitable for each. Remember Mel Gibson's movie *The Patriot*? Remember the scene where Benjamin Martin's (Gibson's) son Thomas is gunned down by the British Colonel Tavington and Martin enlists his other two young sons to lay in ambush for the British detachment? The boys assisted their father in wiping out the detachment, personally killing several of the soldiers themselves. They fired and reloaded their own rifles, but it was Benjamin Martin who did the up-close tomahawk fighting; that weapon wouldn't have been appropriate for the physical size of the boys.

The uproar by the usual suspects over that scene was furious. How dare the movie depict young boys killing, even in wartime! Well, I've got a newsflash for you. That happened a *lot* in those days and continued through the twentieth century. It still happens in justified legal circumstances today, when kids are home alone and someone breaks in. And, until very recently, we had 15-year-old boys lying about their ages to get into WWII and Korea to get a chance to fight!

If your group encounters people armed with weapons other than firearms and not intent upon your personal destruction, they may be dispersed by the brandishing of your weapons and warning them away. Note that the team here tasks the point man with most of the communication, while the others cover their areas of responsibility during the confrontation.

There is nothing wrong with teaching our children how to defend themselves, what a serious and permanent thing taking a life is and when it is justified. Teaching them *all* the aspects of armed defense, including the fact that, under most circumstances, life is sacred and not to be destroyed, is essential. If you don't enlist the help of your children when they are old enough to assist, your plan may not work for long. You cannot sleep with one eye open; rest will be at a premium, fatigue will be in abundance.

Pick a weapon that is appropriate for the small-statured, maybe a

Any able-bodied family member should be an integral part of a survival plan. Here, the author's sister-in-law, Mandy, wields the first gun she'd ever shot and her favorite, the author's 9mm UC9 carbine. It works well for her due to having zero recoil, little muzzle blast or concussion, and 30 rounds of ammo on tap in each of four magazines.

.22 lever gun, such as the ones available through the Henry Repeating Arms Company (Henry doesn't have a blasted crossbolt safety that could mean the difference between life and death in a dire situation), then practice, practice, practice with it. Small but capable children don't need to get a larger gun for a long time, because inside 100 yards, 15 rounds of .22 LR fired accurately is nothing to ignore by anyone. In fact, if you looked at stats, the .22 LR has probably accounted for more deaths in the ranks of civilians than any other caliber since cartridge firearms were introduced. It will do the job, maybe not spectacularly, but the job will be done nonetheless. From there, the new shooter can be taught to at least be familiar with the operation of the other weapons you have on hand. Family members of slight stature may not like shooting your 12-gauge Ithaca M37 defense shotgun in practice, and don't make them do it much, but at least they will know how to work it if called upon to do so in an emergency (and you may assure them that, in the heat of battle, they will not notice the recoil).

How Long Will the Chaos Go On?

No one knows. Localized events depend on the resolution and honor of the people in that particular area. How moral were the people in the area *before* the event? Are they solid, law-abiding folks? How self-reliant are they? Folks in rural, particularly agricultural, areas are very self-sufficient and usually willing to get to work helping their neighbors. Last year, there were numerous tornados in the Midwest, and some of the towns hit were literally wiped out, totally flattened. The folks there didn't go hollering for help from FEMA. They helped themselves and their communities, counties, and states as needed. They didn't even *want* FEMA there, and I applaud them for it. Right now, FEMA has info on its websites, along with the Center for Disease Control (CDC), about what to do in case of a zombie attack. This is not a joke! That's the way to get folks to take a mistrusted federal agency— the same folks who mangled the Katrina response—seriously.

As I tell my police cadets, I don't need to embellish or make up police stories to tell them, the truth is always stranger. The same goes for this book. Indeed, I have to ask, why bother making up stories? Here in the central Ohio area this past spring, state and local EMA held a role-playing practice disaster drill, where the disaster was, you guessed it, a zombie outbreak. What a waste of time, what a joke.

It may be handy to have a less lethal long-range option available, such as the Bates and Dittus UBL 37 37mm launcher. Here the author loads a smoke round in much the same method as a soldier would a 40mm M203 military grenade.

Shame on the local first responders who participated in that ridiculous waste of taxpayer dollars.

The absolute crisis phase of localized, natural disaster-related events (tornado, fire, flood) are usually under control, without looting, in literally a matter of hours. "Under control" means that no one is in imminent danger of serious injury or death. Sure, long-term solutions, such as rebuilding structures and homes, may take days or up to a year,

While the author's wife is totally blind, she is strong and can easily handle the carrying of equipment such as the Food Insurance Essentials Two Week Kit.

and standards of living will be reduced for a while, but supplies and donations from fellow citizens will arrive soon, mostly because, under normal circumstances, Americans are the most generous people in the history of this planet. But if the disaster condition affects a major portion, if not all, of the United States, then we may be talking *years* for full recovery, with certain regions faring better than others.

Therein lies the difference between localized and national disaster. There won't be convoys of food, fuel, medicine, and supplies arriving on a daily basis in national disasters. You will be on your own, like it or not, with only your pre-planning to save you. If FEMA or some other federal agency arrives to help, are you going to want to go to their shelters or food lines? I suggest that would be a bad idea, unless you and your family are starving. Your weapons won't be permitted inside and, in fact, may be permanently confiscated. This is not a palatable choice, since FEMA aid might/will eventually end if the disaster also involves financial collapse or, in the extreme, all the supplies are usurped by some other authority or local tyrant and you end up on your own. How about planning to *always* be on your own from the get-go instead? Then it won't be as big an issue when you are.

Chapter 2

SHELTERING IN PLACE *VS.* BUGGING OUT

W hat plan should you be working on, sheltering in place, bugging out, or a mixture of both?

The answer depends on what the real estate agents always say is important—location, location, location. Simply put, is your home someplace you would want to get *to* or *away* from? The answer to that requires an equally simple set of additional questions: Where do you live? Is your home in the middle of a city? Is the area already high crime? Who are your neighbors? How aware of your neighborhood are outside people, i.e., is it a high-value area that might provide the best return for the least amount of work by marauders?

Next, ask if your home and property can be reasonably defended for a long period of time. Do you have the ability to harden any area of your house? Is there any chance your utility services or any other aspect of modern comfort, safety, and convenience will remain intact, even if it is through your own power generation? Finally, is your home a place you *cannot* leave due to an invalid family member or some other such limiting condition? If your answers to these and other questions point to relocating to a different piece of real estate rather than staying in place, then you will need to be focused on being able to take as many essential items with you as you can, maybe at a moment's notice, leaving behind only non-essential, replaceable items of little *survival* value.

Being able to service your firearm is hugely important. This is especially true with AR systems, which need more care, cleaning, and attention than, say, an AK-type weapon or other piston-operated rifle systems. That's something to consider when you have room for only a select number of tools and you need to get out of Dodge in a hurry. You can only take so much with you.

You can't have too much coverage of any position when the balloon has gone up. Each person in this group has an area of responsibility to provide overwatch of, thus protecting their lead point people as they attempt to accomplish their mission of prying open abandoned buildings in search of food and other supplies.

When is it Time to Go and Where?

Hopefully, some of you have already looked ahead, or thought ahead, and have realized that living in a trendy urban area in the midst of or proximate to a big city with major crime problems isn't the best of ideas. Cops and firemen who regularly deal with the dregs of society have made it a long-standing tradition to live and keep their families as far away from the urban mess as possible. In the rural area in which I live, there are firefighters and cops from both the nearby major urban police department, as well as from many of the now decayed suburban municipalities surrounding the main urban center that used to be considered safe. In my neck of the woods, an average cop with any time under their belt has dreamed of, and sometimes managed to obtain, a "cabin in the woods" on a few acres of defensible land. Those of us who have made this choice are already ahead of the game and are not trying to work our way out of a hole. Cops in particular have been moving out and away from their jurisdictions for the 32 years I have been a cop, but so, too, have many firefighters. Recently, more and more of those cops who have been moving "out" have been doing so not just to keep their families away from day to day criminal activity and other undesirable conditions, but to find a location from which they may be able to withstand a larger societal collapse. This is an entirely new twist on the practice.

If you are hemmed into living in a location near large centers of our population (the epicenters of civil unrest), and you are living in a home that is part of a shared building, such as an apartment or other multi-unit, multi-family condo structure, or a rehabbed or converted factory or warehouse, you will be lucky to just make it out of your unit in one piece. In those kinds of living spaces, the chance of being able to defend yourself against a large number of desperate neighbors or interlopers for any long-term period is very poor, since you cannot protect all sides of your living area or even have visibility on all sides, due to the common-wall construction. If you live in these types of structures, your plan should be for you to leave at the first sign of trouble and know where you are going to go via the safest route.

You Can't Take it With You

This means having to "bug-out" (I hate that term, it sounds silly and overused, and, yes, I know it originated as a military term), or at

Now is the time to be and stay prepared. This includes while vacationing, particularly when you travel by vehicle. This Food Insurance emergency kit should be packed in your vehicle's trunk when you're on the go. Such a kit can get you through being stranded in a remote location while you either wait for help or set out to search for it.

least having emergency evacuation gear at the ready. I won't go into what all should be in the kit in detail, as that is the purview of other publications, including those by Gun Digest. However, I will say that you can't take everything with you! Your gear load is going to be limited by what you can carry on your person or to your vehicle. If you have able-bodied family members or trusted friends and are using multiple vehicles, you *can and will* need to take more stuff. Regardless, if you are carrying gear to your vehicle, you want to try and carry everything you need out in one trip. That may be all the chance you get, and you need to get it right on the first attempt to limit your exposure to attack. There will be things you will have to leave behind, things that can be replaced, and things that are no use to you in the ugly, grim, and dark time that you are facing.

While I have lived by a rule of life that says you can't own too many guns—my wife's opinion non-withstanding, as she says you actually can have too many—when it comes down to it, what are you going to do with that big collection once you need to leave? Remember, your first priority is that you have food, clothing, and water! You won't have room to pack it all, not even all your precious guns, unless you are distributing them to your friends and members of your team for use. You are going to have to leave some of them behind in the best fireproof safe you have or seal them in airtight containers and bury them in a secret location in the event you return later. (You don't want your weapons falling in to the hands of those who may harm you with them later.) So think about what you need to take with you and why you need it. Try to select weapons that can perform at multiple levels, in other words, weapons that are effective at close, medium, and extended ranges. If you must leave a couple behind, fine, but secure or disable them or both. The same goes with ammo and other ancillary supplies.

Who's Covering Your Evacuation?

If you talk to military guys, especially the Special Forces types, of which I'm honored to know a few and am able to seek advice from them, they will tell you two things. First, any evacuation needs to be covered by armed, overwatch support, and second, you can't have too much coverage. Artillery and air power always make nice additions to a hasty repositioning and withdrawal of your forces. Except you won't have the luxury of the air power and artillery thing for the withdrawal of *your* "forces."

Your cover, or "overwatch," if you're lucky, will be maybe one or two people. They could be your spouse, other family members, or friends standing by you obviously armed and watching for anything that is a potential threat while you load the vehicle with gear. They will have to strike a balance between providing an obvious show of force to discourage others, or being behind cover in a low-profile position to protect themselves, you, and the loading team from incoming fire. Once you and your group are in the exit vehicle/s, they will have to cover your convoy as it drives away from danger, which is risky even for soldiers in up-armored HMMWVs (High Mobility Multipurpose Wheeled Vehicles, or Humvees).

The danger and difficulty of evacuating from an epicenter of disorder is not to be taken lightly. Simply being armed is not enough. If it was, no cop would ever have to worry about tactics as they approach a risky situation. The presence of their gun would be sufficient enough to deter attack. What *should* come to mind, if you are in one of these potential epicenter areas and are planning on leaving when things go awry, is to leave before it gets totally and uncontrollably out of hand with as much advance lead time as you are able obtain.

Chapter 3

PRIMARY WEAPON SELECTION

As I began putting the concepts for this book together and looked through my gun safe, as well as through periodicals and Internet writings, I realized there are a least two distinct categories of weapons that should be defined and discussed, as well as a crossover category.

As I watched the various prepper television shows, I saw that some people had made good, solid choices in terms of their armament, while others were going to rely on firearms they had purchased for other purposes such as hunting, target or informal recreational shooting, or defense of home or self during "normal" times. In fact, some of the choices made were, for the lack of a better term, just plain bad, guns that wouldn't hold up to what they were going to be asked to do—providing protection from large groups of angry people who are armed with similar weaponry themselves. So, in order to help get you on what I consider to be the right track, let's look first at what I believe to be suitable survival gun requirements.

Six Basic Requirements

There are six basic requirements that a firearm suitable for tactical preparation must meet.

RELIABILITY — This may seem to be a no-brainer, but, from what I've seen, it sometimes gets overlooked because of other factors that come into play, including the "looks cool" or "My buddy said this is the best!" concepts that may prevent those who are just starting to explore survival weapons from making a better choice. Throw in bad advice from inexperienced gun shop "commandos" and you may not only be on the verge of wasting a bunch of money, but also of making a choice that could affect your ability to survive armed confrontations. To put it succinctly, your tactical preparation guns must, I repeat *must*, be absolutely drop-dead reliable. Every time you pull the trigger, you must get the proper *bang* with the appropriate projectiles leaving the muzzle.

Reliable right out the box the gun came in is best. I don't like guns that take a relatively long break-in period before they can be considered reliable. In this age of CNC machining and with the modern materials that are available, I don't feel there's a lot of legitimate excuse for break-in periods. Detroit and other auto manufacturers gave that up years ago; some of you youngsters reading this don't remember having to drive your new car at different speeds for certain amounts of mileage, the breaking-in period, so the engine would last longer. Give me a weapon that runs flawlessly, right from the box, without doing anything to it. I don't care how trendy or popular the gun is in whatever circle or how much of a status symbol it may be to own, neither is of value for this purpose. If we suffer a national implosion, a finicky firearm isn't gonna get it. If you have to make an emergency evacuation, who are you going to get to fix that fancy (or extremely inexpensive)

Ithaca Gun Company in Upper Sandusky, Ohio, is an excellent example of a modern manufacturing company producing affordably priced, American-made weapons of complex design by relying on CNC Machining. If they tried to make the Ithaca Model 37 on the machining tools of the past, the price would be prohibitive and the tolerances and quality would not be the same. Because of quality manufacturing processes Ithaca utilizes, its guns are ready to go, right out of the box and without break-in.

gun when it goes down? It isn't likely there will be a gunsmith in the crowd of angry, dangerous people attempting to surround you and your family who will volunteer to fix your weapon so that you can go ahead and defend yourself with it.

RUGGEDNESS — Your preparation gun needs to be able to take a beating without functional damage, especially guns intended for evacuation or travel. They need to hold up to lowered levels of maintenance by you, because, unlike our military, you won't have an unlimited supply line from a rear echelon to keep you and your gear up and running. Your weapon choices should not be a type that will require replacement parts like new springs every few thousand rounds or other specialized service for the duration of the conditions.

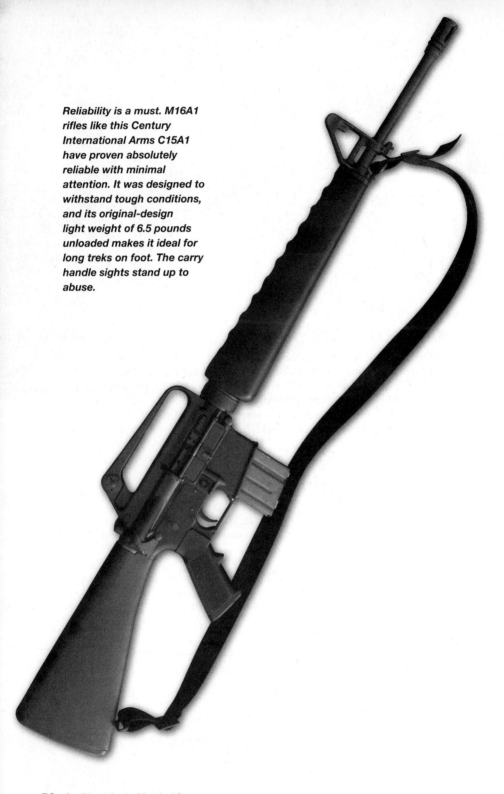

Reliability is a must. M16A1 rifles like this Century International Arms C15A1 have proven absolutely reliable with minimal attention. It was designed to withstand tough conditions, and its original-design light weight of 6.5 pounds unloaded makes it ideal for long treks on foot. The carry handle sights stand up to abuse.

The survival AR-15 is distinctly different than one set up for dynamic entry and use by a tactical team, such as is this Armalite SPR Model 1 with Trijicon ACOG RMR Combo Sight, Surefire Scout Weapons Light, and Grip Pod Systems Vertical Foregrip/Bipod Combo. All these items are great additions to a tactical rifle, but they might not be desirable on a catastrophic survival rifle.

PORTABILITY — When I talk about survival conditions, I don't mean conditions one might encounter on a weekend Audubon Society bird-watching hike. I am taking about dirty, dangerous, painfully brutal conditions, conditions where you will be short of food, water, and medical supplies because of limited carry capacity. Too, you may be injured or ill.

I will be 55 later this year. While I feel I am still in good shape, carrying heavy things around on foot over long distances in terrible conditions doesn't appeal to me much anymore. So, do you think I'm going to want to lug around a fancy, piston-driven, heavy-barreled

M4-type carbine with its acres of Picatinny rail and every accessory under the sun mounted on it for hours per day, maybe for multiple days? How about the excellent and capable Springfield Armory M1A SOCOM II, which weighs in at 10 pounds without anything attached to the rails? You think you can handle it now, sitting there reading this from the comfort of your armchair, but check with me after a day or two of dragging around these kinds of guns under the conditions I'm describing.

Here's a related story from the Vietnam War era. A detective I had the honor of working with at my first law enforcement agency was a Vietnam combat veteran, as were several in our ranks. It really was a privilege to work with those guys and learn from them. They were some of the best cops the U.S. ever had. Anyway, Howard told me that, when he got in-country, he really didn't want to carry the M16 he had been issued; he'd heard about the gun's early unreliability issues. He'd run across another soldier carrying a .45-caliber WWII-era Thompson M1 submachine gun. He traded this guy his M16 along with some other undisclosed items for that reliable Thompson, which seemed to be an ideal jungle-fighting weapon with its .45 ACP bore. In actual combat, I'm sure it was. What Howard soon found out, though, was that the Thompson alone weighed about 11 pounds, not including spare magazines and ammo, quite a load to heft com-pared to the 6.5 pounds of the M16. It wasn't too long before he'd realized his mistake and went about unloading the Thompson on an-other unsuspecting soldier in exchange for an M16. The combat load of a Thompson just wasn't something he wanted to hump around in the jungle all day. Indeed, the weight of the Thompson, along with its complexity in manufacturing, finally did in the Thompson as a frontline combat arm.

Anything that reduces as soldier's combat load, as long as it

The original M16 and M16A1 were the best examples of a battle rifle that did it all and accomplished its mission. It was lightweight, ergonomically designed, and wore rugged sights that doubled as a carry handle. There was also a short buttstock that fit well even while the shooter wore armor. Clearing rooms and buildings with it was easily done. It was the longer, heavier M16A2 that created the need for the shorter, adjustable stocked, lighter weight M4 Carbine.

The M1 Garand was indeed, at one time, "The greatest battle implement ever devised," as it was praised by Gen. George S. Patton, Jr., during WWII. It's shown here with a single eight-round En-bloc clip loaded with 150-grain FMJ ammunition, and the shorter knife-style bayonet that replaced the original sword bayonet after WWII. If offered less reach than its predecessor, but was certainly more versatile in the field. As great as the Garand was, it is heavy, and the eight-round En-bloc clip is ejected with the final round fired. This makes this formidable weapon less than practical for cross-country carry, mostly because of losing clips during firing. It will, however, serve well for long-range defense while sheltering in place.

A full-stocked Auto-Ordnance AOM130 reproduction M1 Carbine shown with a reproduction sling and buttstock ammo pouch. While the pouch is designed to hold a 10-round stripper clip in each compartment, it will also allow a 15-round magazine to be squeezed in each side. The AOM130 does not come with a clamp-on bayonet lug, but one can be added. The gun is shown with a SOG Tactical Tomahawk and Beretta 92 on a military gunbelt. This setup makes a great lightweight survival rig for traveling on foot. Of course, the AOM130 or any .30-caliber M1 Carbine would work for sheltering in place and addressing any mid-range threats.

doesn't reduce effectiveness, becomes favored frontline gear. It is for these same reasons that the weapon/s you choose for guns to be used in an emergency evacuation must be light and easily maneuvered. This also means that some great guns that work for shelter-in-place situations won't cut it for emergency evacuations.

The reverse can just as easily be true. For example, my all-time favorite rifle is my M1 Garand, which was manufactured in 1942, arsenal-refinished once, and given a new walnut stock by a previous

Arms such as Barrett's .50 BMG make outstanding long-range specialty arms for sheltering in place. Pictured at right is Barrett's 107A1 CQB in .50 BMG. Shorter and lighter than the original M107 at 35 pounds naked weight, it's still not an emergency evacuation choice.

owner. This amazing example of combat weaponry was purchased for me for my birthday by my father. It is highly reliable, extremely rugged (although I would hate to mar that excellent hunk of black walnut), shoots the all-time greatest and most versatile battle cartridge ever devised (that would be the .30-06, and so my apologies to all you 7.62 NATO/.308 fans out there), and is simple to operate. It is great to have not only for fun shooting, but also for defending my property at extended ranges. In fact, it is one of the *first* rifles I will pick up for that use. But despite my personal attachment to that Garand, I don't want to lug it around over long distances at a loaded carry weight of more than 10 pounds plus a healthy supply of loaded clips (the WWII combat load on an ammo belt held a total of 80

rounds), and whatever other pistol, food, clothing, and gear I would be carrying. If I can save four pounds or more on my primary evacuation weapon, I'm all for it.

Portability also includes maneuverability in confined spaces—vehicles, buildings, concealment/cover locations, etc. While rifles like the M1 Garand or the M1A/M14 can and have been used in the past for close-quarter building search situations, such rifles are not my first choice for those missions. Give me an M16/AR-15 or M1 Carbine any day over the Garand.

SIMPLICITY — The tactical preparation gun needs to be simple to operate in all facets, including loading, clearing, making safe, and firing. This is especially important in terms of getting the weapon to run from an empty and unloaded state, if that's how it's stored. Is there anything in the "make ready" process that you'll easily screw up? There is always something that someone can mess up, but let's choose a system that keeps that potential to a minimum.

So, how quickly can you go from empty to *boom* without injuring yourself or someone else? For me, simplicity also means you aren't hanging bucketfuls of equipment from your tactical preparation firearm. That includes flashlights and most electronic sights. I know I'll catch flack over that statement, but I think that the K.I.S.S. principle reigns supreme here. The more electronic equipment you have on your weapon to rely on, the more likely it is to break under extreme conditions. Yes, I know we use these items on S.W.A.T., and the military makes extensive use of these items in combat, but both those circumstances are *supported* circumstances. You won't be supported in the same way. Your supplies will be finite, and unlike S.W.A.T., your weapons will be in use constantly (even in terms of just being carried). How many different types of batteries do you want store at your home or lug around during travel? How much benefit do you *really* get from that red dot sight?

Don't get me wrong, during normal societal conditions for law enforcement or civilian use and where resupply is not a problem, add whatever additional pieces of equipment you feel you need. But weapons selected for use in conditions of complete societal disruption should be capable of being brought to ready instantly, with minimum action needed on the part of the operator. There should be no knobs to fool with, buttons to push, systems to check, or batteries to test. This is the same principle I use when it comes to recommending police patrol rifles and shotguns for department-wide issue. The guns stay in their basic iron sight format. No electronics are allowed unless the weapon is personally owned and departmentally approved. This way the individual officers not only can decide what and how many accessories they feel will be beneficial to them, but how much additional gear they want to be responsible for. Want this in simpler terms? Your survival gun, unless it is for shelter-in-place long-range precision, should be one you would be able to bury in the ground (in a protective container, of course), come back to months later, dig up, and be able to fire without failure.

EFFECTIVENESS — Survival guns must be effective in terms of completing the task assigned to them. This means that you can only evaluate a particular weapon based upon what it is designed to do in order to judge effectiveness. For example, the 5.56mm AR-15 and its variants work very well for a number of tactical purposes. In terms of dealing with single or multiple aggressors within 300 meters, it is generally very effective. However, if a 5.56mm AR is the weapon you choose to take with you for protection against grizzly bears in the wilds of Alaska, then its effectiveness rating, and your I.Q., would be very low.

If your primary mission is to address single/multiple human threats at ranges within 300 meters, there are a number of possible weapons choices for this purpose. Of course, some choices will be better than others, and there are also weapons that may be selected for this purpose that are totally *unsuitable*, and that's what we are trying to avoid. Effectiveness in terms of a survival firearm used for defensive/assaultive purposes includes its potential ability to hold off, stop, or turn large masses of people away from your position.

Some weapons are extremely effective in stopping single offenders, due to the amount of destructive energy each particular round puts out, but, due to lower ammunition capacities, would not be effective in dealing with larger groups of assailants. For example, in the incident portrayed in the movie *Black Hawk Down*, two Delta sniper team members, SFC Randy Shugart and MSG Gary Gordon lost their lives after they volunteered to protect downed chopper pilot Michael Durant (who was later captured), from hordes of Somali assailants. At least as depicted in the motion picture, the two Delta Operators were armed with 1911 .45s as their secondary weapons, but the ammo supply for the pistols was exhausted in short order. The .45 was very effective in its basic mission of personal-defense, but not in terms of being able to hold off large masses of angry, determined individuals. The lesson here is that, in order for a weapon to be effective for survival, it must have the highest magazine capacity possible.

SUSTAINABILITY — While shelter-in-place guns can be of a wide variety of calibers since you will have room to store plenty of ammo, any evacuation gun should be chambered for calibers commonly available and popular in any locale, in case you are forced to resupply on the move. I love the 6.8 SPC. In fact, my department sniper rifle is chambered in that caliber. But it is not the gun I am going to take with me when I evacuate, even if I had an M4 carbine chambered for it. How many Wally World type of stores carry it? Stick with the calibers that are popular with civilian shooters, law enforcement, and military users, where not only ammunition is more likely to be available, but also magazines for your weapons in case some of your supply is lost. More on caliber selection later.

Shelter-in-Place Guns

Now that you know the basics, think in terms of some specifics. If you have evaluated your living situation and decided you will make a determined stand for the short or long term in a defensible home position, then you will have the most flexibility in the weapons you choose, the simple reason being that, in your home, you can load up on all the support supplies you will need for that gun. Also, the weight of the weapon itself will have little bearing on your decision to use it for defense. Remember that the weapons you select in the shelter-in-place category are all subject to change. If the disaster is a natural one and your home is laid to waste, you're going to have to evacuate with as many supplies as you can take, previous plans notwithstanding. You may not even be able to get to all your guns. If your home is *not* defensible and you have planned to leave your home from the get go, then the weapons you choose must be light and sustainable in the long term. You might have chosen a Barrett MRAD in .338 Lapua Magnum as a long range shelter-in-place weapon—and it's a great one—but it's not one you want to trek over long distances, and it has no CQB (close-quarter battle) value.

The Layered Defense

Layering your defense is a basic principle as old as armed combat itself. It simply means that, ideally, we have different weapons that are particularly effective for different distances. This is likely of greatest importance as you set up your plan for long-term sheltering-in-place. If you are going the emergency evacuation route instead, it will mean that you have fewer specialized weapons that you will need to make work in a wider variety of circumstances, unless you have an exceptional transportation system. Ideally, the weapons selected should cover these basic ranges/conditions:

- **LONG-RANGE** — While our modern military snipers are getting kills out to 2,000 yards or so, this is performance reserved for a few highly trained and exceptional individuals with very specialized rifles, mostly bolt guns. For the average shooter or law enforcement officer, "long range" is anything beyond 100 yards, especially when one considers we're talking about being on the "two-way range," where targets shoot back.

In these situations, a semi-auto rifle equipped with a lighted reticle variable scope of no more than 15-power works extremely well, although certain battle rifles with precision iron sights are also effective. Full-power battle cartridges on the order of .308 or .30-06 are excellent performers for this challenge.

- **MID-RANGE** — Anything from 100 yards down to about 25 yards. Several weapon types come to mind, but basically a high-cap semi-automatic rifle of intermediate caliber reigns supreme.

- **CQB** — Close Quarter Battle, or 25 yards down to eye-gouging distance. High-cap semi-auto rifles, shotguns, pistols, pistol-caliber carbines, and edged weapons are at the forefront here. The intermediate semi-auto rifle, especially with a bayonet affixed, is an excellent choice, as well.

I'll be covering weapons other than firearms later on, but in the next several chapters, let's take a look at the hardware that's the core to this book, the rifles, shotguns, and handguns that make the best options for your survival.

Chapter 4

RIFLE REMEDIES, FULL-BORE AND FULL-LENGTH

If I could have one and only one survival firearm, it should be a rifle. A good rifle is the most versatile and effective weapon you could possibly select. For example, no matter what an individual Marine's specific job responsibility is within the Corps, that Marine is first and foremost a rifleman. That is their foundation, and it should be ours. But which rifle?

There are many, many fine survival-ready and worthy rifles out there. The biggest problem is selecting just which one is best for you. So let's start the selection this way, by asking this question first: Which types of rifles are illegal within the jurisdiction you currently live, if any? If no type is restricted, then your choice is obviously wide open, but if semi-autos are illegal where you live or limited to 10-shot-

The Barrett MRAD would be a great, extreme-range rifle for protecting your shelter or property. While it is not as heavy as Barrett's M107 or 107A1, it is still quite a load. Since it is a bolt-action, extreme-range use would be its forté, but because rapid-fire capability isn't inherent, targets need to be disrupted before they can get close enough to overrun your position. Weapons like this are at the extreme end of extreme-range defense.

only affairs through permanent modifications, then you have some limitations, but are *not* out of the fight.

Since the survival we are talking about is the protecting of yourself against large groups of desperate human beings and not about wilderness survival in the remote stretches of Alaska, then our first and best choice for work from long- to mid-range circumstances is a semi-automatic rifle of a few limited styles (though often from multiple manufacturers). In my opinion, the rifle at the top of the heap, that meets the six requirements I just mentioned is the direct gas impingement AR-15/M16 series of weapons.

The Del-Ton 20-inch A2 rifle is a solid, reliable, Mil-Spec AR. A bit more accurate than an A1 at longer range, it is also a couple pounds heavier, a big downside. On the A2, the carry handle in non-removable, but there is a bayonet lug that mounts the M7 or M9 bayonet. It can be used for mid- to longer-range defense. Detractors of the AR, particularly those basing their criticisms on its early shortcomings, need to give it a rest. This gun has been, with some minor variations in barrel length, stocks, and sighting systems, the primary service rifle of the United States for 50 years. No other shoulder-fired military weapon that can make a claim anything like that and, if you look back at our military history, the military has had a pretty good record of dumping weapons that don't do the job.

Gotta Love an AR

Before you bash the AR-15, let's look at two of the shortest-lived U.S. battle rifles, the 6mm Lee Navy and the .30-40 Krag-Jorgensen. Innovative designs ahead of their times were both. Ready for many years of military service they were not. An even better example was the quick elimination of the .38 Long Colt service revolver from the front lines following its repeated failure to secure the cooperation of charging Filipino Moro natives. In this case, the Colt's sidearm was a technologically superior design married to a physiologically inferior cartridge. The Army dug into its storerooms and reissued the .45 Colt Single Action Army revolver to its beleaguered troopers and, after the campaign was over, the Army ruled that any future military pistol must be of .45-caliber or better. Seeing the writing on the wall, they even waited until a technologically superior semi-automatic pistol was available instead of going with .45-caliber double-action revolvers like the British had. The time to accomplish this transition was relatively short, showed great forethought, and provided our military with a handgun that was the frontline service pistol for 74 years. What I am saying here is that, if the AR-15 were a piece of junk, it would have been scrapped long before this, along with the 5.56mm cartridge.

One of my fellow commanders at our police academy is a Vietnam combat veteran, having served on ambush details of various NVA supply trails during his tour, in 1969. He was issued an M16A1. Although he doesn't talk a lot about his combat experiences, he did tell me that his A1 ran without a hitch and never jammed; by '69, the military had figured out that you did in fact need to clean them to keep them running, and guys in the field had learned all the operational tricks needed beyond what the armorers suggested. Dave said they would keep them relatively clean and, more importantly, kept the bolt carrier assembly slathered with oil (not recommended for the Arctic or powdery sand deserts, but great for steamy jungles). Sheesh, how simple is that?

The AR-15 I've chosen as my primary survival rifle is a model not currently available as of this writing (although a California-compliant, fixed-magazine type still is). It is the C15A1 that was produced by Century International Arms. Using an original surplus M16A1 upper receiver—forward assist, no case deflector, birdcage-enclosed flash suppressor, original triangular handguards, and fool-proof sights— Century added a new 20-inch, 1:9 barrel, a new forged lower receiver, and topped it off with an original, shorter, exactly-right-the-first-time A1 buttstock. I'm here to tell you, this is the gun I would keep if I could keep only one for civil survival. I keep it absolutely stock, just as it came from the factory , and it rides in my personal vehicle as my primary off-duty arm. With it I can respond to active shooters, barricades, warrant service, or entry. The C15 snaps quickly up to the shoulder, swings like a lively field shotgun, can be carried all day with a basic weight of 6.5 pounds (you gotta love that) and, because of the 20-inch barrel, retains the full ballistic potential of the 5.56 round.

If the Marines hadn't gotten their way in the development of the A2 version in terms of adding the longer buttstock, heavy barrel, and over-built sight system (as a corps of riflemen, their reason for the changes wrought was the enhancement of long-range accuracy and so I find no fault with the concept), there would have been much less need for the M4 carbine, which is replacing the full-length rifle in all branches of service.

Other advantages of the 20-inch C15A1 include:

- It is much smoother shooting than M4-type carbines with their short gas tube. There is definitely less abruptness to the operation.

On the left, the Del-Ton AR-15A2, on the right the Century International Arms C15A1. Note the shorter overall length of the C15A1 versus the A2 Del-Ton. The C15A1 has been set up for multiple patrol and entry duties with the addition of an Inova carbon fiber tactical light on a Midwest Industries tower sight rail adaptor. A SIG mini red dot sight has been mounted on the carry handle via a Tapco carry handle rail adaptor. The author used the lightest weight red dot and light available so as not to destroy the near perfect weight and balance of the original M16A1 rifle configuration.

- Heat buildup is not as bad, due to the longer distance that the tapped gasses follow back to the bolt carrier during firing.

- It gives a longer sight radius for iron sights use.

- It gives longer reach with a bayonet mounted.

- There is no fooling with stock adjustment, it is always right.

- If you desire, electronic sights can be mounted on the carry handle or with a forward scout-type system.

- A weapons light can be added with a front sight tower adapter. (Midwest Industries is a great source for these.)

There is one disadvantage for the C15A1 or any basic A1-pattern upper, and that is the lack of a case deflector when the gun is used by a left-handed shooter. If you want an A1-style AR and are left-handed, you will need to secure a bolt-on cartridge case deflector. They mount through the hole in the carry handle, don't obstruct the operation of the weapon, and save your face from being burned beyond recognition by hot brass. Dillon Precision carries them for around $20.

Full-length ARs with the original pencil-thin barrel profile are rather hard to find these days, since everyone seems to want an M4 profile for the advantages they feel they gain with the shorter barrel and adjustable stock. DPMS is cataloging one that is very close to the original rifle format, the A1 Lite 20. Not really a true A1 nor an A2, it is sort of a hybrid. The Lite 20 weighs in at 7.3 pounds (still heavier than an A1, but not by much), compared to the nine-pound heft of the standard A2-style rifle. Weight is saved by using a lightweight barrel and the A1-style carry handle and sight system, which drops nearly two pounds off the basic weapon load is significant. There is a case deflector and forward assist, as well as a bayonet lug. The handguards

The rifle that preceded the M16 in combat in Vietnam was the Colt/Armalite-produced 601/601. Issued with a green Bakelite stocks, the 601 featured a hard-chromed bolt carrier group and prong-type flash suppressor. It lacked the forward assist that was added two generations later to the M16A1 series, and the case deflector that appeared on the M16A2. The case deflector has definite merit, which cannot be said of the forward assist. Left-handed law enforcement M16s need the addition of an add-on to protect the shooters' faces from cartridge case burns.

are the modern round format, and the buttstock is the longer A2 style (can someone *please* start producing A1 buttstocks again?), which is a little long when body armor or heavy winter clothing is worn. In any event, the fixed A1 or A2 stocks have one final advantage over any collapsible M4-type stock, and that is the capability of delivering a last-ditch defensive strike with the buttstock.

While a 20-inch full-size AR is my general preference for a civil survival rifle (I also have the heavier 20-inch A2-style rifle by Del-Ton intended for the same role), the M4-size weapons are also a great choice and can be had in lightweight formats. One basic model that

This Rguns 20-inch Twister Barrel 5.56 upper is mounted on a Sun Devil custom lower. The Rock Ridge bipod and Vortex 3-15x illuminated reticle scope give the 5.56 cartridge the best possible terminal effect at long range. Note the use of 20-round magazines for an extended-range AR; 30-round magazines don't allow the shooter to get low enough to the ground and gain a correct prone position. Bullets weighing 69 to 77 grains are recommended for this type of setup and work well with the 1:9 twist rate this rifle has.

stands out and won't break the bank is also from DPMS, the AP4 Carbine. At 7.15 pounds, the AP4 features the standard military M4 stepped profile barrel, round handguards, military-style adjustable stock, and the removable A3 carry handle for flattop optics mounting. There are loads of this type carbine on the market from loads of manufacturers, with an almost limitless variety of stocks and accessories available in just about any combination possible to imagine.

Here's one piece of advice. For whichever manufacturer you select, particularly in the case of a carbine-style AR. Stick with Mil-Spec construction for your survival gun. Yes, mid-length gas systems on

Officer Shawn Lingofelter test-fires an early example of the Bushmaster gas piston upper. During testing, more than 1,200 rounds were run through the gun without cleaning and, in the end, the action was so clean it looked like it had just been pulled off the rack at the local gun shop. While piston guns keep the chamber clean during fire, there is no standard or Mil-Spec universality with these systems. Each manufacturer uses its own design. Piston guns also add weight and expense to the AR and tend to be less accurate than direct gas-impingement guns.

carbines do shoot more smoothly than the carbine-length systems. I have one on the M4 I used for entry on the SRT team. But the problem is that there is no standardized length for mid-length gas systems. That is what Mil-Spec really means. Besides requiring a certain basic level of quality, it requires that the parts that meet that standard are all the same, which reduces any potential problems with resupply and repair. Until there is a Mil-Spec standard for mid-length gas systems and their ports, save that type of system for personal police duty weapons, home defense in standard times, or recreational shooters. Which brings me to the topic of gas piston ARs.

An M4-style carbine, like the DPMS AP4, in its basic configuration makes an excellent lightweight and relatively compact survival rifle, easily adjustable to fit people of a wide range of sizes and weights.

The gas piston AR is a popular and, perhaps, important technological variation of the original Stoner direct impingement system. The gas piston does one main thing to enhance the AR-15 system: it keeps hot powder gases and fouling out of the action of the weapon. In the original direct impingement system, gas is vented from the barrel through a small tube into the receiver, and it is that gas that blows into the bolt carrier to force it back against the butt-stock buffer and spring. When these are compressed, the weapon cycles and forces the carrier back forward, stripping a fresh round from the magazine follower and into the chamber, where the bolt locks up, awaiting the next pull of the trigger. The action of a direct impingement gun will, of course, eventually be fouled by carbon. (The level and rate of fouling depends upon the length of the gas tube and, more importantly, the type of ammo being fired.) With the short-stroke piston action, the gas is vented from the same area from the fore-end, but instead of being directed into the action, is directed against a piston and rod, which in turn cycles the action. This keeps the action very clean and, in theory, operating more reliably. This is all well and good, but there are several other things a gas piston system does that make it less desirable for the type of survival weapons we're talking about.

First, piston-actions cost more than direct impingement ARs. This extra money can be spent on more ammunition, magazines, or other supplies.

Second, the design of the piston action generally adds up to an additional pound of weight for the weapon (actually for the weapon *carrier*). This is weight that could be traded for an equal amount of ounces in water, food, ammunition, or medical supplies.

Piston actions also tend to cause a given weapon to be somewhat less accurate than a direct impingement gun, due to a sliding assembly of metal moving across the top of the barrel that interferes with harmonics. Every precision AR out there that I'm aware of, especially those set up for sniper use, runs off direct gas for just that reason.

Just like mid-range direct gas systems, no Mil-Spec standard exists for AR piston guns produced for the civilian market. In fact, there are a bunch of different types and setups out there. It is not something that can be easily repaired if it fails, since there are no standard parts. Even without the survival factor thrown in, it's entirely possible that the manufacturer that produced your weapon won't be around to make good on that "lifetime guarantee" they provided to help you.

Despite these drawbacks, piston guns do have their place. If you have a major aversion to cleaning the bolt and carrier group of the AR, are not in a situation where you will have to pack it over long distances, are not concerned about a weapon breakdown in an unsupported area or situation, and are willing to pay the higher the price tag, then by all means get one. If those things don't apply to you, stick with a direct gas gun. In any event, make sure you stick with the 5.56mm round. Like I said, I love the 6.8 SPC, and there are a number of other new rounds out there that show promise, like the .300 AAC Blackout, but they aren't available everywhere and they tend to be more expensive in terms of per-round cost (like $30 for 20 rounds kind of expensive).

From Russia, With Love

There are piston-operated rifles that don't have the same number of drawbacks as the AR piston systems, at least in terms of added cost or lack of commonality. One of the most prominent examples is the semi-automatic AK-47 family of weapons.

The AK-47 weapons, actually the semi-automatic variants of the family, really have only a couple weak spots that prevent them from being considered by me as being the top pick for a battle rifle, the spot I feel is currently occupied by my aforementioned CA-15A1. Let's start first with the AK-47 strengths.

Semi-auto AKs are available nearly anywhere in the U.S., save for those "people's republic" (kind of ironic, isn't it?) areas of the U.S. where any such type of semi-auto rifle is banned. Fortunately, that doesn't include too many places (not yet, anyway). Further, they are far less expensive than almost any decent AR. If your finance's are limited, you are much better off buying an AK, magazines, and as much ammo as you possibly can for the cost of an AR rifle alone.

The AK-47 was designed with simplicity and reliability as its primary requirements. It had to function in the extraordinary weather extremes found in the Soviet Union, which tended to generate loads of mud, dust, snow, and ice, depending upon the time of year and location. It was also expected to function this way in nations within the sphere of Soviet influence, places like Cuba, Africa, and, of course, Vietnam. Not only did it have to function in those extremes of climate, but also in extremes of abuse, neglect, and ignorance. Mister Kalishnikov knew full well who the end users of his design would be. Even in the once mighty Soviet Army, the level of education and training wasn't the highest, with many of its ranks coming from rural peasant society. So the Bloc's weapon had to be simple enough for even the most uneducated person, without access to tools, to field strip and maintain. Thanks to the AK's long piston operating system, which assures that the action stays cleaner than the direct gas impingement AR-system, Kalishnikov accomplished his goal in spades. The AK is the most widely distributed firearm, for better or worse, in the world.

The AK is chambered for what I consider to be the ultimate intermediate battle cartridge, the 7.62x39mm. If the 7.62x39mm could be made to function with absolute reliability in the AR-15, there would have been little or no need for newly introduced rounds like the 6.8 SPC or .300 AAC Blackout. As of this writing, though, Rock River Arms has introduced an AR with adaptations that will allow it to

Today's American-made semi-auto AK-47 Sporters from IO, Inc., feature excellent synthetic stocks and lighter weight than wood-stocked versions, especially the AKs with milled steel receivers; the Sporter's is stamped steel. The Sporter carries very well and, for the author, rides next to a Maxpedition Sitka pack. A built-in mounting point for a scope or red dot sight is on the left side of the receiver.

The IO, Inc., AK, in spite of some nice upgrades, is still capable of having a standard military AK-47 knife-bayonet mounted on it. The AK-47 bayonet is especially handy in that its sheath has a mounting point that allows it be used as a wire cutter. The American M9 Bayonet copied this capability.

operate reliably with this round, the Model LAR-47. I did not have the opportunity to test it for this book, but I can tell you that it stands a good chance of exhibiting superior performance, due to the fact that it accepts standard AK-47 magazines, not modified AR-15 mags. While it does hold promise, its MSRP is $1,200, which could pay for two decent quality AKs instead.

If an AK becomes your choice, stick with the 7.62x39mm over the 5.45x39mm. The 7.62 is more effective generally than the 5.45. (The Soviets introduced the 5.45 in their war in Afghanistan, replacing it with the 7.62 before they left. Guess that says something.) Ammo is universally available and inexpensive, and an AK chambered for

7.62x39mm will function with any commercial or military ammo you feed it. It is simply not ammo sensitive. Just stick with the non-corrosively primed brands. To me the cost savings of buying corrosively primed ammo just isn't worth the extra work to clean the gun afterwards.

The AK's overall length is short enough that it is ideal for any mission from open battlefield conflicts to room entries. Folding stocks are available, and they do shorten the gun's overall length considerably, but they aren't necessary for shelter-in-place guns. For use as a travel firearm, the folding stock allows the use of short gun cases that have less attention getting profiles.

The single biggest disadvantage of the AK versus the AR weapons system is the AK's less than sterling reputation for accuracy. When I say this, I only mean that you can't just pop a scope on an AK and turn it into a designated marksman weapon, something you very nearly can with an AR. Its accuracy, however, is more than enough for the battle conditions it has been used in for the past 65 years. So, instead of a 1.5-inch or less group at 100 yards that you can produce from about any AR, you will probably be looking at three- to four-inch groups. There are several reasons for this.

The tolerances of the AK are not as tight as those on an AR. On the other hand, this is, in part, what accounts for its reliability and ease of maintenance.

The second drawback is the gun's iron sights. They are open in style and not as precise as the peep sights found on the AR.

Overall weight of the AK is at least a half-pound greater than the weight of a basic M4 AR carbine. Models that have the milled steel rather than stamped sheet metal receiver models will weigh even more.

The operational controls, well, frankly, they stink, at least in terms of their ergonomics compared to the AR's. The AK safety,

This folding stock AK by Century Arms can be wielded in and fired from an automobile with the stock in the folded position. Very handy when you're runnin' and gunnin' to save your life.

Test-firing the Century International Arms Polish AKM with underbarrel folding metal stock revealed that, while the metal stock is not quite as comfortable as a wood or synthetic one, it works well and is actually more than tolerable. It is very compact with the metal stock folded underneath, far more so than a 16-inch M4-style carbine with the stock collapsed. Unfolded it extends out to the full-service AK-47 length.

in particular, is the biggest headache. Kalishnikov had economy of manufacture in mind as part of the design. So, instead of having a separate ejection port cover or something that protects the inside of the weapon from getting mud in it, the safety, when on, also covers the receiver cut that allows the bolt handle to be drawn to the rear. It's clever (two functions, one piece to manufacture), but it makes it comparatively difficult to operate. Your fingers can't reach it without releasing your grip on something. Also, releasing an empty or full magazine requires the full-time attention of an entire hand, rather than just the use of a single finger, as with the AR. With an AR, your thumb has to hit the paddle release while it removes the magazine.

While these last two problems can be mitigated with practice, when it comes right down to it, running an AK just isn't as fast as running an AR. On the other hand, no one who has ever faced an AK in combat, to the best of my knowledge, has ever reported any deficiency of the opposing force in terms of being slow to continue to deliver firepower, nor in terms of reloading or getting the AK into action against them.

In talking with one of my Army Special Forces operator friends about his opinion of the AK, accuracy was the only downside he could see for this weapon. Still, the accuracy issue is one that only becomes readily apparent when it comes to the vast open spaces of places like Iraq and Afghanistan. For jungle fighting or inter-urban combat, where ranges are not likely to be greater than 100 yards, there is very little practical difference between rifles that can hold 1½ inches or four inches at that distance. There's even more validity to this argument when you are on the two-way range, where stress will defeat your ability to fire accurately, at least in the opening phases and until your adrenalin dump becomes a positive factor, rather than a negative one.

In working with semi-auto AK variants from IO (the polymer-stocked Sporter Model) and Century Arms International (the underfolding Polish variant), I have come to a better appreciation of the AK. There is a lot to be said for one that is of reasonable quality. While the BATFE regulations that require a certain amount of American-made parts be added to the mix—40 percent, I believe—seem very silly on their face, I think it has added an additional level of quality to the weapons, as opposed to the AKs that were strictly imports prior to the 1994 Assault Weapons Ban. If I couldn't afford the AR of my choice, I would be totally comfortable with one of these partly American AKs as my primary survival guns despite their two operational deficits of looser accuracy and a tedious safety system.

There is only one other concern that I have for the AK as a survival gun in current times. It is only a theoretical issue, but one often mentioned. The AK is clearly seen as the "bad guy's gun." Due to its low cost and its ability to deliver a high volume of firepower, it is very often the weapon selected for use by criminals such as drug traffickers and active shooter. (Of course, that same low cost is the reason so many recreational shooters who just like to fire a lot of rounds on the target range purchase them.) What's worse is that it's the weapon the liberal news media portrays as being responsible for the crime problem in its entirety. Because of this, certain police officers who are not gun enthusiasts themselves will view the possession of this type of weapon with suspicion. Now, in the case of total chaos, this won't matter, but in current times it might. This means that you must be very careful in terms of legality and visibility if you travel with an AK in pre-disorder times. It is just a factor of its rather ill-portrayed reputation that will require a bit more attention on your part in order for you to travel with one without issue.

Ruger's Ranch Rifle

If you want a weapon with piston operation reliability but don't, for whatever reason, wish to use an AK-47 variant, there are still some other excellent choices available. The next one that comes to mind is the excellent Ruger Mini-14.

The Ruger Mini-14 has been around for a very long time. It was considered a premier law enforcement patrol rifle for those very few agencies who would allow them, primarily because it shot the .223 Remington cartridge rather than a pistol round, and it was far more available and less expensive than Colt's Model 1 Sporter. I once borrowed a personal Mini-14 from a state trooper friend of mine when I was a detective on our drug unit and was tasked with checking, by myself, a rural location used by devil worshippers; devil worship was considered a major threat, in 1983. The Mini-14 was convenient to carry and provided an extra measure of comfort when I located the site, which did appear to have been constructed for its alleged task.

I purchased my own a year later. It was full hardwood stocked, in blued finish (the stainless model wasn't available yet), and had the hardwood upper fore-end cover, instead of the more efficient, yet uglier, fore-end upper that later became standard. It was a handy rifle, and it was thanks to this rifle that I discovered the .223 round was far more powerful than rumored at that time. It never missed a beat. Unfortunately, that particular rifle is on the list of the ones that I let get away, being traded for something else I felt I needed more.

The Ruger Mini-14 was the first rifle issued to our patrol sergeants at my sheriff's office in Union County Ohio, as a field test of the advantage of the patrol rifle over the shotgun. Turned out it was a *big* advantage in our wide-open, flat, farmland patrol area. By that time, we were issued the stainless steel, synthetic stocked variants and Nitrex-coated steel magazines. Over the years of supervising annual qualifications and training with these guns, I've never seen one malfunction or have any other issue. In fact, they would have been the standard patrol rifle for both sergeants and deputies alike, had it not been for the Department of Defense Law Enforcement Assistance Program, which provided our agency and many others with M16A1 rifles for just the cost of shipping. Still, even with M16A1s in hand, several of the supervisors, including the Chief Deputy of the sheriff's office, elected to stick with their Ruger Mini-14s.

The Mini-14 offers several great advantages for those who select it, and it would be another top pick if I didn't already own several AR-15s.

For starters, the Ruger Mini-14 is patterned after the operating systems of the M14 and M1 Garand, two service weapons whose reliability is beyond reproach. Using investment casting, Ruger managed to build a scaled-down version with some small variations, the most noticeable being that the placement of the trigger guard is slightly to the rear of the action, rather than beneath it as it is on the parent rifles.

Like I said earlier, the Mini-14 runs and runs with little attention. According to Shawn Herman, the gunsmith at Vance's Shooter's Supply, in Columbus, Ohio, the Ruger Mini-14 is one of the guns that doesn't come back to him in need of repairs. Truly, I believe that it would have become the dominant 5.56mm law enforcement (LE) rifle had it not been for 1). the DoD program, and 2). the fact that all the Desert Storm and Iraq/Afghanistan war vets who have been filling our law enforcement ranks had not been already so familiar with the AR operating system. Not to mention the greater versatility of the AR platform, but I digress.

The open-top action design of the Mini-14 allows one to totally view the entire action when the slide is retracted. The chamber is totally visible and accessible for everything from an emergency clearance (not likely) to a quick field cleaning. On the AK and AR, one can see only a portion of the operating area without a field strip and, even then, the direct view of the chamber area is limited.

The Mini-14's safety, which was debuted on the M1 Garand, is truly ambidextrous. It is located inside the front end of the trigger guard ahead of the trigger and is pushed forward to take off safe, pushed in to safe, and is clearly visible from both sides of the rifle. I also like the gun's sight system, which is rugged, simple, and low profile.

The Mini-14, in original configuration, is a lightweight rifle. I favor the blued steel model listed as the Mini-14/20 Ranch Rifle, which comes with a 20-round magazine and hardwood stock. Wood is nature's camouflage material. We really didn't need much camo in the pre-synthetic stock days. At seven pounds, it is a tad heavier than the black-stocked synthetic variant at 6.75 pounds, but I prefer the wood variant. Need more camo? Put some camo wrap on the barrel. In any event, it is lighter than many of the M4/AR-15 variants out there. The tactical variants of the Mini-14 can add up to a pound to the gun and $60 to the cost. By way of comparison, the Standard Model of the Ruger SR556 M4-type piston driven carbine is a pound heavier than the Mini-14/20 and costs *$1,000 more*, which is pretty much the price for any piston-driven AR. You can sure purchase a lot of gear for that kind of money.

Unlike the AK-47, the Mini-14 is not considered a "bad guy's gun," particularly in the wood stock version. Remember that the Clinton Assault Weapon Ban of 1994 targeted "Black Guns," the synthetic-stocked models and guns like the AK, which were tactical black in color and had bayonet lugs on them (massed bayonet charges being a common criminal gang tactic at the time—*not*). The Mini-14 was still produced after the ban, but only with five-round magazines (even though 10 would have been legal, Bill Ruger, Sr., didn't want to draw any more attention to his company). For years, 20-round magazines were hard to come by. Fortunately, with a change in company direction, Ruger once again, though long after the sunset of the Clinton gun ban in 2004, began producing 20-round magazines for sale to civilians. If five-round factory magazines were still the only type available, I might have been a little hesitant to recommend the Mini-14, unless I'd been able to find a quality brand of reliable aftermarket magazines.

The Ruger Mini is popular and well distributed nationally, but stick to the .223/5.56mm chamber. For a short period of time, this rifle was also marketed in 6.8 SPC caliber. It would not be a choice of mine for a survival gun. Too, the Mini is also available as the Mini-30, which is chambered in 7.62x39mm. It is up to $100 more expensive than the 5.56mm model (Ruger recently went from .223 to the 5.56 chambering). The Mini-30 is only available with synthetic stocks, and overall the gun is not as commonly encountered as the Mini-14. I did not have the opportunity to test one, so I can't comment that it has the same level of reliability as the 5.56 version, but I haven't heard any reports to the contrary.

There are a couple disadvantages to the Ruger Mini-14, just as there are for any weapon. First, the accuracy level, at least in the newest versions, lies between that of an AR and an AK, depending on the load used. Accuracy has been improved recently, due to the use of new CNC machines in the plant in Prescott, Arizona, which produces a more precise weapon; previous generation Mini-14s produced accuracy more like the AK, which was still adequate for most patrol work. Barrel twist for the Mini is 1:9, which allows for the widest range of 5.56mm bullet weights.

My other nit-pick with this gun is that the mounting of optics is a bit more challenging on the basic models. The UltiMAK company offers railed upper fore-end replacements that allow the forward mounting of scout-type optics. However, in keeping with the survival weapons philosophy, an optic really isn't needed, or even particularly desirable, especially since the Mini-14, with the exception of the cumbersome Target version, would not be at its best at extreme long range.

An Oldie But Goodie

Next on the piston-driven list for use at medium and CQB range is the very tried and true M1 Carbine, specifically the new versions produced by Auto-Ordnance Corporation (Kahr Arms). If you have a WWII original, feel free to use it, but if it is one that is truly a collector's grade, you may not want to deploy it at just this moment. That's where the Auto-Ordnance guns come in.

Operating under the short-stroke system developed by Winchester and David Marshall "Carbine" Williams, which differs from the long-stroke system of the M1 Garand in that it is not actually connected to the action via linkage, but rather strikes the action open as does the modern AR piston system. The M1 has proven from WWII through Vietnam to be superbly reliable. Further, its 5.5-pound weight makes it the lightest long gun to serve in frontline combat, even though it was never intended to be there (it was supposed to be used by support troops and rear echelon ranks). However, its light weight and high magazine capacity (15 rounds, at the time) made it very popular with troops who were limited in logistical support, such as paratroopers. A special version, the M1A1 with a folding stock, was produced for them, making their combat load even more compact, a handy quality when exiting the door of a C47 aircraft wearing a parachute and all the other survival gear needed to operate

This Auto Ordnance AOM 150 M1A1 Paratrooper Carbine is the author's favorite model. Featuring excellent ergonomics and enough walnut to be aesthetically pleasing, it is a versatile and reliable weapon, capable of serving either as a travel gun or for sheltering in place. Note the 30-round M2 Carbine magazine. The M1 Carbine is often disparaged because of the power, or lack thereof, of the .30 Carbine cartridge. True, it is not the .30-06, the round it was compared against in WWII and Korea. But it does have 600 more foot-pounds (ft-lbs) of energy at the muzzle than the 9mm fired out a pistol, and only 300 ft-lbs less muzzle energy than the 5.56mm. Within the ranges we are discussing, it will certainly do the job and do it very efficiently in terms of weapon weight and recoil. The ammo is compact and takes up very little space compared to the larger cartridges it is often up against.

behind enemy lines. The M1 Carbine would have been an even better weapon if it had been first introduced as intended, as the full-auto M2 Carbine, but the military wanted to save money at first and introduced it as semi-auto only. The M2 didn't appear until after WWII and saw extensive use in Korea.

Fast forward to Kahr Arms and its acquisition of the Auto-Ordnance Corporation. Auto-Ordnance had, for a number of years, kept the semi-automatic version of the Thompson submachine gun alive, along with a rendition of the 1911 .45. At the time, its 1911s were not known for great quality or reliability. All that changed when Kahr took over. Not only was there an improvement in the firearm quality, but also an expansion of the product line with the addition of the AOM130 full stock M1 Carbine and the AOM150 Paratrooper folding stock version.

The M1A1 Paratrooper version is one of the handiest weapons of its type and power level. The folding stock doesn't actually lock, but, when opened, it remains firmly in place. Unlike other metal folding stock systems, it is extremely comfortable to fire with, in part due to the leather cheekpiece, but also due to the almost non-existent recoil of the .30 Carbine cartridge.

Neither the AOM130 or 150 come with bayonet lugs, as the AOM130 are modeled after the early M1s. The sights are the early, non-adjustable peep sights, and the safety is the crossbolt push-button type, a style that was later replaced by a rotating lever type. Price is reasonable. The standard magazine shipped with either is a single 15-rounder, with 30-rounders available from Kahr.

I outfitted both the 130 and 150 with a sling and plan to add a bayonet lug in the future. Either carbine possesses the advantages of extremely light weight and reliability, plus they have the advantage of naturally camouflaged walnut stocks.

The M1 Carbine, whether the newly manufactured series by Auto Ordnance or the original WWII version shown here with bayonet affixed, still makes an excellent survival gun in urban areas or rural areas of broken country. Wide-open areas such as America's overrun Southwest border may tax the carbine's effectiveness. Consider it a 200- to 250-yard weapon under most circumstances.

The M1 Carbine has little or no identification as a "bad guys gun," as it was not included in the Clinton 1994 Assault Weapons Ban. That is subject to change, as President Obama is preventing the return of M1 Carbines and the M1 Garand into the U.S. from South Korea. With that in mind, for the moment, today's Auto-Ordnance

M1 Carbines are reasonably priced compared to WWII M1s, nearly all of which are now collector's items.

The only disadvantage to the M1 is in terms of accuracy at longer range. This is due to the short-for-caliber round-nose bullets that are chambered in factory loads, the piston system of operation, and the fact that this weapon was neither intended to be used as a primary fighting tool, nor fired at the distances the M1 Garand was set up for. But, for mid-range to CQB distances, especially by smaller family members who don't like recoil, this weapon is hard to beat.

The Bigger Big Boys

There are two other piston-operated rifles that deserve mention, especially for longer-range defense, where a cartridge with greater punch is called for, or where a larger weapon is easier to support as a shelter-in-place weapon. Those guns are the M1 Garand and the Springfield Armory M1A.

If you have never shot either of these rifles, you don't have an appreciation for the capabilities of the full-size battle rifle. I have owned and fired my Garand for several years now and know that, if I shelter-in-place, as is my current plan, this will be one of the primary weapons I'll deploy to deal with any threats approaching my house at ranges greater than 50 yards—especially if that threat is vehicle-borne.

Ball ammo .30-06 opens vehicles like a can opener. I used it as a comparison (okay, I actually brought it out for fun), when we were deciding on 5.56mm loads to use in our department's new M16s and had been provided a Pontiac GrandAm for just that purpose. While the 5.56 rounds would punch through the driver's side door and into the passenger side door, dimpling the outer skin but not penetrating

The Savage 110 Tactical .308 Carbine is a five-shot bolt gun that would do for long-range defense, though it is limited in capacity and speed. Factory equipped with an Army Digital Camo stock, the Carbine is shown with a Vortex scope and bipod. The tactical carbine is lighter than many sniper rifles currently available.

it, the Garand sent its round whistling through both sides, throwing up large showers of dirt upon impacting the bank on the other side.

Much as I appreciate that gun, if I have to leave, that beloved Garand would stay behind, unless there was someone who needed it. That choice is due to its disadvantages.

Not only is the M1 Garand limited to eight rounds of ammo in its en bloc clip, but when that eighth round is gone, so is the empty clip, and you may not have time to recover it. (Conversely, box magazines can easily be recovered when empty, a topic coming up in the training section of this book.) In other words, in short order you could end up with a single-shot weapon. Other than that, it is an excellent long-range weapon even without a scope, is reliable to a fault and, like the Mini-14, possesses the form of a safety that it passed down to its progeny, which includes the M14/M1A.

Long-range semi-auto domination can be had with a custom rifle like this .30-06 M14 tack driver from LOSOK custom arms in Ohio. The weapon is fed from a slightly modified 20-round Browning BAR magazine.

Its attributes aside, the Garand is *heavy*, a full 11 pounds when loaded up. God bless our guys who lugged it around during two wars! Of course, they also had the advantage of being kids during those wars, which I, unfortunately, no longer am. It is also a long weapon, one designed for open battlefields, not house-to-house fighting.

Want the power advantages of the M1 Garand without the clips? Then the Springfield Armory M1A is for you, if you can afford it. At around $1,700 it's pricey, but it solves the eight-round en bloc clip issue of the Garand and gives you a 20-round box magazine in exchange. It also retains within 100 fps or so the power of the .30-06 in the form on the 7.62 NATO (.308 Winchester) round.

While the M1A solves the en bloc clip issue of the Garand, it is still a long and relatively heavy rifle. The standard walnut stocked version weighs in at 9.3 pounds unloaded and is 44.33 inches long. The length and weight can be mitigated somewhat by selecting the walnut-stocked Scout Squad, which shortens the overall length by four inches, but somewhat unfortunately maintains the same weight as the full-length version, likely due to the addition of a Picatinny rail on a metal upper fore-end handguard. If you want more length and weight removed, you can go with the original SOCOM 16 version, which drops the weight down to 8.8 pounds and the overall length to 37 inches. This is accomplished not just by shortening the barrel, but by adding a synthetic stock. This makes the M1A applicable to long-distance carry and room-to-room CQB. Don't select the SOCOM II. This well-intentioned variant turns the M1A into a 10 to 10.25-pound behemoth, a weight just not worth the effort for survival purposes.

Chapter 5

SHORT STUFF: SCOUT RIFLES, LEVERS, AND PISTOL-CALIBER CARBINES

During the late 1980s and early '90s, before it was realized that the 5.56mm loaded with expanding bullets (like the ones Hornady's TAP loads wear), weren't the over-penetrating dangers for police work they were once thought to be, pistol-caliber carbines were viewed as the answer for light-recoiling, reliable, semi-auto weapons that would extend an officer's effective range to between 100 and 150 yards. Marlin produced a recreational sporter during that period called the Camp Carbine 9, and later the Camp Carbine 45, both of which were simple blowback, wood-stocked weapons never intended for police service. But they were pressed into service, much like the M1 carbine, because nothing else was available, and because the 9mm version used either Marlin-supplied or Smith & Wesson Model 5906 pistol magazines. As a number of police departments were

The Century International Arms UC-9 9mm Carbine, shown here and on the previous page, is an excellent travel gun. While it is possible to fire it one-handed like a pistol, such firing should be in a dire emergency, as from a vehicle. Firing from the shoulder with the stock extended produces good accuracy to 50 yards. Note in the top photo on the previous page that the 9mm UC-9 is backed by a Beretta 92 in the Bianchi Universal Military flap holster, a smart move that keeps ammo consistent across multiple firearms.

using the 5906 high-capacity 9mm duty pistols, they realized that officers could fuel their carbines with the magazines already carried on their belts. (The .45 version used 1911 single-column magazines of any manufacture.)

When the Marlin started to become more popular, Ruger jumped into the fray with the PC9 and PC40 carbines. Built with black synthetic stocks, both guns were far more robust and suitable for police work than the Marlin guns, which had virtually disappeared after the assault weapons ban of 1994 anyway; Marlin likely decided to go back to concentrating on making lever guns and avoid any chance of controversy. The Ruger guns were also blowback weapons and used Ruger magazines from the P Series of semi-auto pistols. The problem there was that few agencies issued or permitted Ruger semi-autos as duty guns, so the magazine advantage was mostly nonexistent. As good as the PC9 and PC40 were, they fell out of favor when the expanding .223/5.56mm rounds started hitting the law enforcement market and government M16s became available. The two Ruger carbines are no longer cataloged or manufactured, having quietly been deleted from the Ruger inventory.

There are three pistol-caliber carbine-type weapons truly worth considering, especially for a vacation or travel gun. One is the Century International Arms UC-9. The UC-9 is made from an assortment of genuine UZI parts and assembled here in the U.S. It has a 16-inch barrel, is semi-automatic (having been converted to fire from a closed bolt instead of from the original open bolt of the full-auto UZI submachine gun). At nine pounds, the UC-9 is no lightweight, but in return you get a mostly steel weapon that makes handling even the hottest 9mm rounds an effortless task. Yet the gun is very compact at only 24 inches overall with the stock folded, and a mere 31.5 inches with the stock extended. The UC-9 provides a lot of close-range firepower within that package and, according to the online catalog, comes with two, 32-round all steel magazines. However, the hard copy of the catalog says it comes with four magazines, which my sample did.

The UC-9 is one of the few pistol-caliber carbines worth owning. It makes a great travel gun, due to the fact that it can be fired with a closed stock from, say, inside a vehicle if surrounded, or opened up full length for longer-range fire, out to 100 yards or so. The sights, while original, are rudimentary, as they were designed for a very short-barreled weapon to be used primarily at CQB distances. However, the longer barrel and closed-bolt operation gives it added versatility and likely increased accuracy over the submachine gun version, and the trigger is long but easy to operate. This is a special-purpose weapon indeed, but one that's easy to fire. In fact, this gun was the very first firearm my sister-in-law, Mandy, the photographer for this book, ever fired. She did very well with it, and it was a great introduction to shooting for her. It is an excellent choice for the recoil-sensitive members on your team. I was surprised to find that Mandy favored it over the four-pound lighter Auto Ordnance M1 Carbine. Value for this weapon is great. I found it for sale, new—technically the UC-9 is not a "new" weapon, as it's a mixture of new and old parts, condition very good to excellent—for $771 with five magazines.

Other advantages to the UC-9 besides the compact size include the blowback action, which on one hand makes it heavy for its size, but on the other makes it extremely simple in terms of construction. There simply isn't much to break, and what is in there is rather massive. It is also easy to clean and maintain. Downsides besides weight and the sights? If you did want to add things like sights and optics, it would be hard to do, as there simply isn't much out there for it. You can pretty much forget rails, other than something you could clamp on the barrel. Then again, that's not what you want, right?

The final downside I can see is simply limited effective range, due to the 9mm cartridge. You are probably effective, at the most, out to 150 yards. The 9mm might surprise you though. I can stand with my Glock 17 at 100 yards, fire two-handed, and put six for six rounds in the qualification zone of a state silhouette target, *without* holding over at that range. With full-power duty ammo, it's a flatter shooting round than it's usually given credit for. I can highly recommend the UC-9 as part of your survival armory.

Another pistol-caliber carbine (sort of) still in production that I can recommend, one that gives greater range than a standard pistol round, one that is far more compact and lightweight than an M4 with the stock collapsed, and one whose design is stellar in terms of having truly ambidextrous ability, is the 5.7x28 FN PS90 carbine.

According to the FN manual, the PS90 is a blowback-operated bullpup carbine firing from a closed breach. It weighs 6.61 pounds (which is really deceiving, since it seems *much* lighter, undoubtedly due to its small size), and has a maximum width of 2.3 inches and an

A team member with a UC-9 folding stock carbine provides rear guard security. UC-9 magazines hold 30 rounds of 9mm.

The FN P90S Carbine is a unique, if somewhat expensive, CQB to mid-range compact carbine. Totally ambidextrous to the point of possessing back-up iron sights on both sides of the built-in optic, the blowback action never seems to miss a beat. Terminal effect of the 5.7x28mm commercial soft-point rounds are on par with the Winchester 9mm Ranger +P+ round fired from a pistol. A horizontal clear magazine mounted on top holds a whopping 50 rounds!

overall length of only 26.3 inches. The basic/original version has a fixed optical sight integrally mounted. There are many advantages to this carbine and only a couple disadvantages.

The PS90 is the only firearm I've worked with that is truly and naturally ambidextrous in operation, with the disk-shaped safety capable of being operated by the trigger finger of either hand, pulling it toward you to fire if you are right-handed, and pushing it away from you if you are left-handed.

Cartridges are fed through a translucent, amber colored polymer magazine that sits flush on top of the stock, but underneath the sighting module, parallel with the bore and chamber. Release the magazine by operating either of the two magazine releases on either side of the magazine at the chamber. This keeps the weapon very compact, with no protrusions to catch on anything, and allows the shooter to keep track of the status of the 30 to 50 rounds in the magazine (depending on the version you have). Reloads are slower than with an M4 or a weapon with a box magazine in standard position, but with a full 50 rounds on deck, you may not need a quick reload at all. Ejection is downward through the large ejection port, located aft of the pistol grip portion of the weapon. No empty casings will hit your face, no matter which way you hold the weapon while firing, so no case deflector is required.

The weapon is charged by grasping one of the identical, ambidextrous cocking handles located on either side of the barrel assembly and pulling directly backward. There are two separate sets of backup iron sights on either side of the optical sight, one for right-hand shooting, one for left-hand.

The blowback system of the PS90 is totally reliable. There is zero recoil and very little muzzle blast, due to the 5.7 cartridge and the PS90's integral flash hider. There is nothing else like it out there.

The disadvantages of the PS90 are few and can be gotten used to with a bit of experience. The fixed Optical Ring Sights sighting system on the base model, for one, isn't adjustable—at least there's no adjustment method described in the manual or visible on the sight. Upgraded models now have a Picatinny rail system that allows the user to mount an optic. I did find the ORS sighting system effective after working with it long enough.

I also found the trigger to be spongy, but that's typical of a semi-automatic bullpup long gun. It did, however, work well enough for defensive purposes.

Originally, ammo availability and price were issues, as only FN (FNH USA here stateside) provided civilian-legal sporting loads. That has changed, FN production is at full tilt, and other manufactures market this capable little round now, too. In ballistic testing, it proved to be as effective in test medium, in terms of width and depth of the permanent wound channel, as the 127-grain +P+ Winchester Ranger 9mm ammunition fired from a pistol.

Another drawback is that the PS90 is pricey, with online prices running from $1,700 to $1,900 from various sources. You will have to decide if the price is worth the needs you feel this weapon will meet.

A fellow cop friend of mine, a guy who is so committed to his preparation that I consider him a real expert in the overall picture, discussed with me his preference for the Kel-Tec SUB-2000 Carbine, a gun he carries in a basic backpack with several magazines. A 9mm or .40 Smith & Wesson carbine that folds in half for extremely compact storage, the SUB-2000 can be configured to use various types of magazines, therefore making it compatible with your primary handgun. My buddy has his set up to run off of 9mm Glock 19 or 17 magazines (he has some 18-rounders), but the 9mm version is also able to utilize S&W Model 59, Beretta 92, and SIG P226 magazines. The .40-caliber version can be purchased to run off of Glock 22 or 23, Beretta 96, S&W 4006, and SIG P226 magazines. The magazine well is located in the pistol grip, like the UZI weapons family.

Weighing only four pounds unloaded, the SUB-2000 folds from an overall length of 29.5 inches down to 16 inches. Note that this is an "out of service" storage length, i.e., the weapon cannot be fired from its folded position. This is because the gun is, in a manner of speak-

The 9mm Kel-Tec SUB-2000 is one of the most compact and concealable long guns on the market. While it cannot be fired when folded up, it can be kept in very small cases or backpacks. Here and on the following four pages you see the SUB-2000 as my friend and survival expert "Bill" travels with it, tucked behind a seat in his vehicle. The gun can be brought into action very quickly and allows the shooter to easily address threats out to 150 yards.

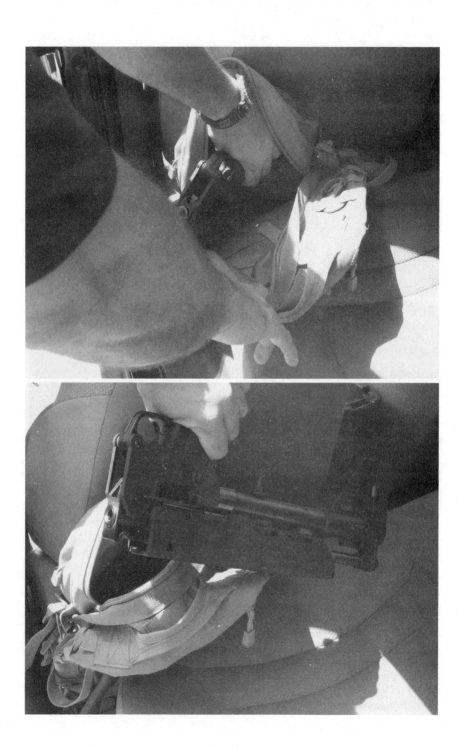

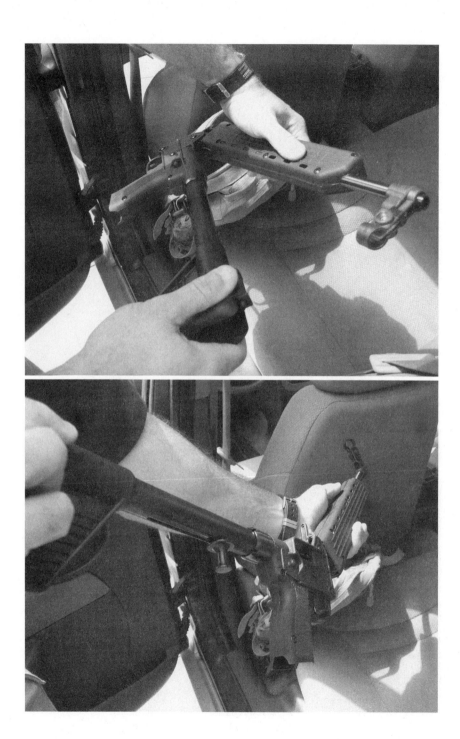

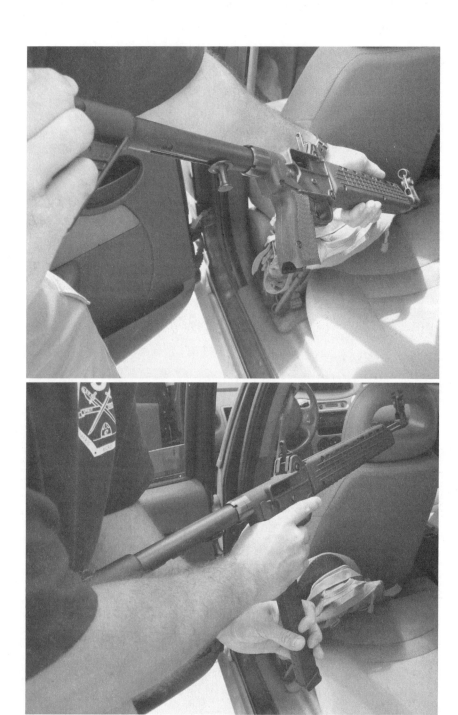

ing, partially disassembled when folded, that is, it is out of battery and cannot fire until it is locked open again. If it could fire while folded, its overall length would be longer than 16 inches. By comparison, the Auto-Ordnance M1A1 Paratrooper folding stock carbine, which *will* fire with the stock folded, is 25.75 inches long overall. Considering that the SUB-2000 is only 4.74 inches longer when locked open (and it locks open *very* quickly), the inoperative folded condition really doesn't pose much of an operational issue in an emergency.

With an extended 18-round Glock magazine, my friend has a lot of longer-range firepower available in about as inconspicuous a package as one can imagine. Plus the price is right. Note that Kel-Tec also has a 5.56mm version of the same concept, the SU-16, but, due to the nature of the rifle and its operation, its folded out-of-service length is much longer at 26.4 inches. Personally, if the out-of-service length is the same as some of the folding stock weapons out there that can be shot while folded, I will tend to want to go with the folders.

Long-Range Weapons

Long-range rifles for shelter-in-place defense can be of multiple configurations, including bolt guns. Although bolt-actions are not my first choice, if I had one nicely set up for sniper use, I wouldn't give it up. But I also wouldn't buy one. I want repeat-fire capability. Right now, my duty sniper rifle features a Sun Devil Manufacturing lower combined with a Stag Arms Model 7 upper in 6.8 SPC, a cartridge with "just right" ballistic performance at extended range. Set up with a Vortex Scope, Harris Bipod, and 20-round magazine, it has great precision.

By the way, Stag Arms is now featuring a 2012 Executive Survivors Kit that features the following items for just over $2,000 complete. The setup includes a Stag Arms Model 2 AR-15 rifle with

Diamondhead Versa-Rail handguard; EoTech 517 Holographic Red Dot Optic; a Stag Arms Field Repair Kit; an OTIS AR-15 Cleaning Kit; a Silent Sling; two 30-round Magazines (10 rounds for restricted states), and 60 rounds of quality ammunition of undisclosed brand.

That's a great package, but what also makes this an emergency survival kit is the inclusion of other survival items. These include: a set of Gerber MP 600 Multi-Pliers; Gerber Omnivore LED Flashlight; a dual-purpose human/pet first aid kit (nice touch for the pet inclusion part); an MRE field ration meal; and a Pelican 1700 long case. While this kit is not complete, it is a start and the components are kept in one place, which would be good for travel (although water needs are not included). If anything, it shows how prominent the topic we are discussing here has become, and manufactures are catering specifically to this segment of interest (although sometimes they are more interested in upping their profit by bundling things you may not need). At least the concept is solidly out there. From there it's up to you to evaluate the things that writers such as myself and product manufacturers have to say, see if it makes sense and, most importantly, see if it works for you.

In any event, remember this. Most mobs, if they are not somehow extremely determined or composed of religious fanatics (such as the Mogadishu mobs in the *Black Hawk Down* incident, who were also amped up by the drug "khat"), will likely be turned back with very few rounds, especially if you can pinpoint the leaders or primary agitators. Most groups intent on looting would fall into the easily turned category, at least until they become desperate from starvation. Any setup remotely like mine will work well for you, including direct impingement .308 ARs, such as the SDMR variants. One such example would be the .308 LRT SASS rifle from DPMS, which was recently selected as the new, primary sniper rifle by the Columbus

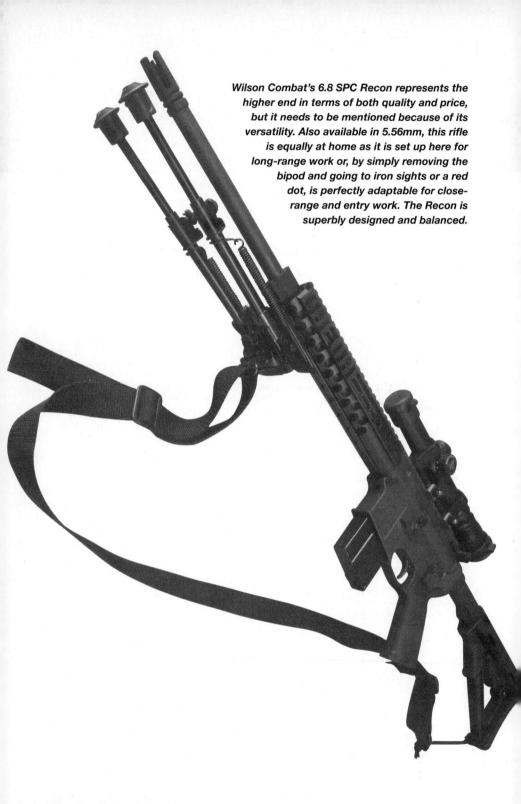

Wilson Combat's 6.8 SPC Recon represents the higher end in terms of both quality and price, but it needs to be mentioned because of its versatility. Also available in 5.56mm, this rifle is equally at home as it is set up here for long-range work or, by simply removing the bipod and going to iron sights or a red dot, is perfectly adaptable for close-range and entry work. The Recon is superbly designed and balanced.

A custom-built .30-06 semi-auto based on the .308-caliber M14/M1A action. The author used this rifle in a recent counter-sniper school to great effect. Magazines can be converted from Browning BAR magazines to accommodate the longer .30-06 rounds.

Police Department S.W.A.T. team to replace the Blaser bolt-action sniper rifles now relegated to backup status as they are phased out. Select what you can best afford and fire accurately, but select quality for the long haul.

Alternate Action Platforms

What if you can't legally possess what the news media calls "assault rifles" in the jurisdiction in which you live, but still want some modicum of longer-range firepower that's comfortable to shoot, like the AR, AK, or M1 Carbine? Or what if you regularly travel to areas where these weapons aren't looked upon with favor and you want to keep a lower profile, even though possession of the semi-auto guns wouldn't be illegal. The lever-action rifle may be your best option in these scenarios.

While I've said that our own M1 Carbine could be considered the very first assault rifle (lightweight, compact, firing an intermediate cartridge), it is actually the first *semi-automatic* assault weapon. Looking back, the 16-round lever-action .44 Rimfire Henry Rifle, as deployed in the Civil War, could be seen as an assault rifle, at least in concept. While it wasn't compact or lightweight by any stretch, it was referred to by Confederate forces who faced it as "that damn Yankee rifle that you load on Sunday and shoot all week." Compared to the muzzleloading .58-caliber Springfield Rifle, it was quick firing and quick loading, due to its use of an actual copper-cased self-contained cartridge of adequate close-range power. A number of Union soldiers armed with this personally purchased weapon could easily overwhelm opposing Confederate forces armed with their single-shot Enfield rifles.

I know we don't face single-shot muzzleloaders much these days in massed charges, but the lever gun still has potential. One I favored for examination was the Marlin 1894C chambered in .357 Magnum/.38 Special. The 1894C is a trim, handy firearm, actually compact enough for close search activities, yet accurate enough for somewhat longer-range use, especially when firing .357 Magnum cartridges. Using either .38 Special or .357 Magnum loads, you can generally expect a 200 to 300 fps improvement in velocity over what you'd get from a four-inch barreled revolver. Plus you get a magazine capacity of nine to 10 rounds, depending on which cartridge you choose and which bullet is loaded in that particular round. I prefer this version over the .44 Magnum, because the .357 Magnum recoil is considerably less, allowing for the fastest possible follow-up shots. Let's take a look at some of the other pros and cons of this gun.

Power range in the area of the M1 Carbine, but because it fires the same rounds a .357 revolver does, your ammo supply can pull double-duty. It's also legal to own anywhere that firearms are legal to own, and the price of the weapon and ammunition is reasonable.

Not much ever goes wrong with Marlin lever guns. A bigger plus is that, unlike a detachable pistol or rifle magazine, you can't lose the feeding system, because it's part of the gun.

This last point is also one of the gun's disadvantages. The tubular magazine is slower to reload that any box magazine-equipped

Here the Marlin 1894C lever-action rifle is backed up by a classic, nickel-plated four-inch Colt Python .357 Magnum; if the threat is up close and personal and the 1894 is empty, retain control of the situation and go to the handgun. Right off you'll notice the Marlin is lightweight, has excellent handling, and can be fired rapidly without removing it from the shoulder; bolt guns are a little more difficult to accomplish this last task with. The iron sights are good and easy to pick up, thanks to the brass bead at the front. I also like that it's a multi-caliber weapon (.357 Magnum and .38 Special) without modification and fires readily available cartridges.

Lever-action rifles like the .357 Magnum Marlin 1894C are trim, fast handling, and pack a punch. What's best is that even when shooting full-power 158-grain .357 Magnum rounds, recoil is mild compared to the experience of shooting the same loads through various revolvers. The carbine holds 8+1 rounds of .357 Magnum, and 9+1 rounds of the even milder shooting .38 Special. It makes a great weapon for defense where semi-autos are currently illegal, as well as a great choice for smaller-statured shooters. Another plus is that there are no box magazines to lose. The downside: reloading through the port is slow.

firearm. The gun itself is also more difficult to make safe and totally clear. From a maintenance standpoint, detailed field stripping isn't going to happen, the gun just wasn't designed that way.

With regards to effective range, here it would be considered limited compared to the .30-30, although magazine capacity is higher (there's a trade-off for everything). Generally, expect effective defense distances to be in the 150- to 200-yard range. Hornady's Flex Tip LEVERevolution ammunition may extend that a bit, but this weapon is not in the same class as 5.56mm firearms.

The Marlin Model 1894C lever-action rifle (top) and the Mossberg 590A1 pump-action 12-gauge shotgun are both are good for travel in areas where a semi-auto shotgun may not be welcome due to local laws. Spare ammo is a must, and the BLACKHAWK! 90-round bandolier gives a shooter a good amount of it. As for the rifle, spare .38 and .357 ammo carried in their original boxes can be dumped in a pocket or satchel to reload from when things get interesting. Loading out of loops is slower than loading loose rimmed cartridge ammunition.

I saved mentioning bolt-action rifles until last. While I realize that bolt-actions were the primary arm of the majority of all armed forces soldiers in WWI and WWII, they are not the most desirable weapons in terms of support during times of civil upheaval. This is simply due to the low magazine capacities of most. In terms of real, combat-capable bolt guns, not sporting guns, the 1903 Springfield, 1917 U.S. Pattern Enfield, or the German Mauser are three guns that are the ultimate bolt-action rifles in terms of reliability under battlefield conditions—but you're stuck with a fixed, five-round magazine capacity for them.

There are a great number of recovered WWII German Mauser rifles out there at a most reasonable cost. They are superb rifles, but they are chambered in 8mm Mauser (a great, full-power battle cartridge), which is not the most commonly available military rifle round out there. One bolt-action battle rifle that gives you more magazine capacity is the 10-shot .303 British Enfield. These rifles are still available in shootable condition and are reputed to have a very smooth action. But, again, we have the same problem with them as we do with the German Mauser, that being that the .303 British round isn't readily available. In fact it is easier to find 7.62x54R rounds for the Russian Mosin-Nagant in quantity and at a low price than it is to find 8mm or .303 British ammo (plus the Russian guns are available at lower prices than any of the others mentioned).

If I had any of these guns and could afford nothing else in terms of survival guns, I would hang on to these and stockpile ammo. If I really felt I wanted to rely on a bolt gun for defense and wanted one of modern manufacture, though, I would look at the Ruger Gunsite Scout Rifle.

Chambered in .308 Winchester and available in both right- and left-handed versions, the Gunsite Scout, unlike other previous scout-style permutations, is equipped with a 10-round box magazine. And, while Steyr and Savage versions also sport box magazines that are removable, they aren't of a 10-round capacity (there is a Steyr adaptor available to allow the use of 10-round magazines), and the Steyr is very expensive. I saw one online with a Leupold Scout Scope for $2,400. Ouch.

The Ruger Gunsite Scout follows the late Col. Jeff Cooper's vision of the ultimate survival rifle, a gun that could be called upon to do just about anything under any condition. From surviving alone in the wilderness, defending yourself from two- or four-legged predators, or taking game, a scout rifle should be counted on to do it all. Ruger's take on it is unique I think. Additionally, this rifle is capable of holding 10 rounds of .308 Winchester right off the bat with no adaptor needed, and the price is reasonable, with an MSRP of $999, a far cry from Steyr's offering.

There are several other positive features that might commend Ruger's Gunsite Scout as a survival firearm. The weight is a very reasonable seven pounds. The stock is listed as being "Black Laminate" wood, although it looks a tad grey. I would like to see laminate color options in tan, walnut, or green also available. Laminate wood is very tough and isn't subject to the same level of warp as a standard wood stock.

There is a very thick recoil pad, which is helpful in a lightweight bolt gun like this. Peep sights are standard, and there is the forward Picatinny rail section for the forward-mounted scout-style scope. For those of you not familiar with this, a scout scope is set up with pistol-length eye relief and a power no greater than 4x. This allows one to keep a good peripheral view of any threats in the area, since the scope isn't right up against your face. The receiver retains the standard grooves for mounting Ruger scope rings and an optic. Leupold makes the best example of the scout-type optic.

In addition to the Picatinny rail, the barrel is topped off with a Ruger Mini-style flash hider, which I think is a nice touch. All the metal with the exception of the bolt and handle is black. Unlike the Savage version, which is a good gun but only has a four-round magazine, the bolt knob is of standard size.

Action is of the controlled-feed Mauser style, a critical feature for a battle rifle. Barrel length is 16.5 inches, making the Gunsite Scout adaptable to both CQB and long-range situations. Because of the bolt-action, there should be no ammo sensitivity issues. On the downside, magazines aren't commonly available. If you can find them, stock up.

Bolt guns are problematic in other ways. User-friendliness is an issue. In order to cycle the action, you need to break your firing grip and trigger position entirely. This, in part, is what causes this action type's biggest disadvantage, a slow rate of fire. While this isn't a problem when taking out targets at ranges past 100 yards, closer in this isn't the case. From a standing position, most shooters will end up dismounting the gun from the shoulder while cycling the action. It is for this reason alone that both law enforcement and military snipers are now switching to semi-auto AR platforms for their sniper work (plus the AR has been enlarged to .308 by several makers and accurized right at the factories). This change was born of the target-rich sniper environments of the Middle East battlefields; the bolt gun just couldn't keep up or protect a shooter's position when discovered.

If you can overcome the slow rate of fire with other weapons and shooters, the Ruger Gunsite model is a battle-ready choice for survival situations. It is one that can handle a fairly wide variety of situations and one that won't break your bank or your back.

Perhaps offering the best balance between power and size, the Springfield Scout Squad provides the user with a shorter barrel than the standard M1A, enhanced flash suppression, and a section of rail for optional scout-style optics mounting. Its stock is available in the miracle camouflage material called wood.

The Bayonet

From about 1989, when democrats in Congress began pushing for the assault weapons ban they eventually got passed in 1994, during the Clinton administration, guns with bayonet lugs were viewed as being among the most evil type. I lobbied with other cops from across the U.S., on multiple occasions with the NRA and the now defunct Law Enforcement Alliance of America, against such a ban for those five years and was shocked by the level of hatred that existed against rifles with bayonet lugs.

By that time, I had been a full-time cop for around 10 years and had never seen a bayonet charge by gang-bangers or any other criminals. Be that as it may, the presence of a bayonet lug on a rifle like the AR, AK, FN, or SKS (where the bayonet is removable but built in), was one of the items that, if present on a gun in combination with other "horrible" features such as flash hiders and a magazine greater than 10 rounds, prohibited its new manufacture, import, or sale. Thus, the bayonet lug was ground off many of these types of rifles from 1994 to 2004 so as to make them saleable—all this, *even though a rifle with a bayonet affixed to it had never been used in any sort of crime* (not even during the great Los Angeles bank robbery of 1997).

Little thought has been given to the bayonet since that time, other than by collectors of certain weapons. Now is the time to look at them again, but not quite for the purpose they were originally designed.

Starting in late WWII, the bayonet changed in form and function. Prior to that time, most military bayonets were almost a type of short sword, with a blade roughly from 10 to 17 inches in length. This length gave the soldier maximum reach for thrusting through their opponent when battle was close or ammo was low. However, bayonets of those lengths, or the spike-style bayonet on the SKS, weren't really good for a whole lot of other uses, and the tool spent most of its time adding weight to a soldier's belt.

As WWII progressed and the M1 Carbine found itself in unintended frontline combat service, there arose a cry for a bayonet that would fit it. Due to the short length of the carbine itself, the old-school, full-length sword bayonets unbalanced the gun severely. In answer, the M4 bayonet was introduced, along with the barrelband bayonet lug. The M4 bayonet was much like the Ka-Bar fighting knife made for the U.S. Marines, right down to the leather washer handle (Korean War versions were produced with plastic handles). With a 6.5-inch blade length that could be sharpened of both sides, the bayonet no longer was a little-used burden for a soldier to carry, but became, instead, a piece of equipment that could be used as a bayonet, fighting knife, or a tool for prying or opening rations and other items.

Starting in 1953, the 16-inch-long M1905 bayonet (which fit both the M1903A3 Springfield bolt-action rifle and the M1 Garand), and the 10-inch blade M1 bayonet designed by John Garand for his M1, were replaced by the knife/bayonet M5. The M5 used the same blade as the M4 and was equipped with a plastic handle. This is the model I have for my M1 Garand, and it's handy. But even if I didn't have the rifle to go with it, the M5 would make a great survival tool in and of itself.

The advantages of the knife bayonet were not lost on the rest of the world's armed forces. When the AK-47 replaced the SKS, the folding spike bayonet was replaced by a knife-style bayonet, and armies of the world followed suit in a similar vein with the new weapons they introduced.

Today's armies don't tend to use bayonet charges as part of their standard tactics, although soldiers are still taught basic thrust-and-parry fighting techniques with fixed bayonets. This makes sense, as the bayonet was designed to be affixed to the muzzleloading single-shot rifles in standard use by the world's militaries of that era, intended to be used as a "reload" when the armies closed with each other. One of the more recent examples of the bayonet's deployment was in a charge by the 7th Cavalry in the battle of Ia Drang Valley during the opening phases of the Vietnam War. There the troops were ordered by Col. Hal Moore to fix their M7 bayonets on their M16s in the final battle for control of the valley.

History is history and useful at that, but use of the bayonet on our survival rifles is not for bayonet charges. Where the bayonet shines is for use as the ultimate weapon retention device while moving on foot beyond your defensive position. There are many long gun retention techniques taught to law enforcement officers in order for them to safeguard and control their guns (although my method would likely be a pull of the trigger). Even though some long-range accuracy may be degraded by the addition of a bayonet, any close-quarter gun grab would be stopped in its tracks, and if the grab attempt was originally a surprise, the bayonet's presence would allow time to adjust, remove a safety, and fire any needed shots.

The modern bayonet is of course, a knife, and a tough one at that. If you have a rifle that can accept a bayonet, find one, either a good used one or a new reproduction model, and make it your survival knife. That way you maximize the utility of the weight of this particular tool that you'll be carrying. (Anything you'll be carrying for emergency evacuation use should have as many uses as possible for it to earn a space on your body.)

One particular bayonet that does this is the newest M16 bayonet, the M9. There are a number of manufacturers who make this bayonet, who's design is really focused on its use as fixed-blade survival knife, since that is the most likely use for this tool in an army that probably has to ask for permission before they affix it to their weapon (can't look too mean and aggressive these days in war, right?) Anyway, the M9 is much upgraded over the M7 in that a wire cutter attachment has been added to the scabbard tip in a fashion similar to the design on the AK-47 knife/bayonet.

The M9 makes a very fine stand-alone survival/camping/outdoors knife, even without the rifle to go with it. Note that the M9 can be added to properly equipped Mossberg 500/590 shotguns, as well, which helps address those firearms' lower magazine capacity a bit. Beyond the M9, for survival purposes, consider that any rifle that can mount a bayonet should have one available for it. For example, if you have one of the Auto-Ordnance M1 Carbines, a barrelband bayonet lug can be added to it with little effort.

A sample of twentieth-century combat bayonets. From left: M7-M16 bayonet; an AK-47 bayonet with built-in wire cutter attachment on the sheath; a leather "washer handle" M4 bayonet for an M1 Carbine; a Korean War-issue M5 knife bayonet for an M1 Garand; and an M1905 sword bayonet for a 1903 Springfield rifle.

The dual threat of a powerful rifle and fixed bayonet is perhaps the ultimate in intimidation for close-range confrontations. Bayonets affixed to M1 Garands were an integral part of 1960s and '70s riot-control methods used by National Guardsmen, not for the purpose of conducting bayonet charges, but rather for keeping rioters at bay and preventing the Guardsmen's rifles from being taken without firing a shot.

Survival use of the bayonet as a long gun retention device is seen in this sequence. Here, a defender who is armed with a five-shot 1903 Springfield .30-06 rifle equipped with the 1905 sword-type bayonet is surprised by an unarmed attacker seeking control of his weapon. Instead of gaining control, the attacker is seriously injured for failing to take the presence of the bayonet into account before making his move.

Above: M4-style carbines produced after the sunset, in 2004, of the 1994 Assault Weapons Ban, such as this DPMS AP4 held by this defender on the left, come equipped with and can mount an M7 or M9 bayonet, just like full-size M16, M16A1s, A2s, A3s, and their semi-auto counterparts.

Top left: This AO AK Sporter supports the standard Kalishnikov bayonet, as does the Century International Arms folding stock variant.

Bottom left: The addition of the M4 bayonet on the M1 Carbine will buy this defender several seconds of time if rushed from close range, allowing him to shoot, create distance, or even thrust with the bayonet. Auto Ordnance M1s pattern early issue Carbines and so do not come with the barrelband bayonet lug in place, although they can be added later.

Chapter 6

SHOTGUNS, A TOP CHOICE FOR CQB
(CLOSE-QUARTER BATTLE)

The shotgun has merit as one of your survival weapons, although I wouldn't want it to be the only one available in the civil disorder scenarios we are talking about. For most wilderness survival, farm and ranch utility duties, or home-defense situations it is an outstanding tool, and you could do just fine if it was the only weapon you had for those purposes. It can be useful, too, during civil chaos, and while it shouldn't stand unsupported, it is a good mid-range and close-quarter battle (CQB) weapon in many situations. Of course, if it is the only weapon you have or can afford, like so many other things in life, you make due. Having a shotgun for defense is certainly better than throwing back the rocks hurled at you by the mob that wants to tear you and your family apart.

You're looking at the main reason the shotgun, in this case a 12-gauge Mossberg 590A1, is still a viable weapon—the .72-caliber hole it makes. This is a view no attacker wants to see.

Many of you don't remember this, but short-barreled shotguns, starting with the 1897 Winchester pump, used to be known as a "riot" shotguns, terminology I'll use here for this weapon type. This was back in the day when it was still alright for cops to shoot lead pellets (rather than rubber), at people who were causing mass property destruction and injury to others. Today things are different, and not necessarily for the better. Civilians today are preparing for a time when those situations won't be happening in a far off city or to unoccupied businesses. It will be happening to us, everywhere and in every corner of the country, not just the big cities, and there won't be any cops around, myself included, to drive those looters off with rubber bullets, tear gas, and water cannons.

There is only one type of shotgun that should be selected for the task of riot gun and that is the pump. The pump gun is simple, fast, reliable, and can digest *any* ammo of the proper gauge and length you can find. The semi-auto is much more complex to operate, more expensive, and more likely to be sensitive to different power levels within a gauge range. Too, other than the recoil-operated Benelli shotguns, the majority of semi-autos will require more maintenance and cleaning to continue their functionality. That is why police agencies never went to semi-auto duty shotguns *en masse* and limited their issue to specialized units like S.W.A.T.

The riot shotgun should be of the type termed the "tactical shotguns," which I cover extensively in my book *The Gun Digest Guide to Tactical Shotguns*. The barrel length should ideally be 18 inches. A 20-inch barrel will also work, but 18 is best. Twelve- or 20-gauge models are the gauges that will work best. Leave the .410-bore out—it simply doesn't have enough longer-range power for riot duty outside the home. The 20-gauge has more than enough power but with less recoil than the 12-gauge, which means faster follow-up shots. Don't worry about needing a flash suppressor or compensator on the barrel in either gauge. You or another selected user should be able to handle one without compensation, and if that's not possible, then get a different weapon. Also, don't worry about going through all the BATFE paperwork and obtaining the NFA tax stamp for a shorter-barreled version. You lose too much in terms of ballistics by going shorter than 18 inches.

The bore should be choked Cylinder or Improved Cylinder. Don't waste money on a gun with an interchangeable choke system. Those are for sporting use and, in addition to racking up the cost, mean parts that can be lost or, worse yet, used with the wrong type of ammo. It would be a bad thing to shoot rifled slugs through a shotgun wearing a Full choke, for instance.

The riot shotgun should have a tough protective coating, Parkerizing or some sort of matte finish, and be a model in common use by our military or civilian police forces. A quality riot gun made by a recognized manufacturer is not that expensive compared to most AR-15s. Don't try and skimp by purchasing a bargain basement model from a questionable overseas source for your long-range survival needs. It won't hold up to the tasks you're going to ask of it. Do not, I repeat, do *not* get a shorty pistol grip-only shotgun without a buttstock. A folding stock is okay and is useful for defending yourself from inside a vehicle, but don't forgo a buttstock altogether.

Let's talk a little bit about the pros and cons of the riot shotgun for survival use.

Top on the pros list is that the riot shotgun is at its best when used for mid-range and close-quarter defense of one's home, shelter, or vehicle, from about 25 yards and closer in to what I call "eye-gouging distance." The effects of being hit by multiple large

The shotgun still has a place as a CQB or mid-range weapon. Here the rear guard is armed with the excellent Mossberg 590A1, a Mil-Spec shotgun with adjustable stock.

pellets at the same time at the ranges I've just described are documented and legendary. In fact, few other civilian legal weapons are as effective. The only conventional weapons likely more effective are full-auto bursts fired from submachine guns or military rifles like the AK-47 or M16.

These are versatile guns. The riot shotgun can be loaded with 00 Buckshot for defense against large angry mobs or large angry animals, or with field/hunting loads for use in the emergency taking of small game. Indeed, my riot shotgun became a standby weapon after I found my neighbors were keeping two female lions in the house I rented to them next door (yes, you read that right). Until they moved out, I kept one with me often when letting out my dogs and my wife's guide dog. Plus, at least when it comes to people, the large bore and the sound of the pump's action being operated have always been intimidating to the bad guys. It shows you mean business.

Speaking of versatility, shotgun ammo is absolutely universally available in both 12- and 20-gauge chamberings, some would say in an extreme of variety, and even in areas of the U.S. under the most stringent gun control. Buckshot of various sizes, birdshot of various sizes, rifled slugs, sabot slugs, duplex loads, signal flare rounds, less-lethal rubber pellets, and projectile-free stun rounds are readily available at retail shops and through specialty outlets online. There are even low-recoil shotgun rounds available in both buckshot and slug offerings.

Stay away from the really bizarre rounds, such as chain and flechette rounds. These projectiles are unpredictable in flight (part of their charm) and are usually made of steel, so it is possible to ruin your bore with them. Truthfully, there is really nothing that can be done to make the shotgun more effective than it already is when used with standard round lead pellets—and there certainly is *not* enough of an improvement to warrant the extra expense or risk in using exotic loads. If you were to shoot someone with those exotic rounds now, in our current pre-collapse days, you will face some hard questions in court, such as "What made you feel that a standard loading of 00 Buckshot wasn't deadly enough for your home- and personal-defense? Were you really defending yourself or were you seeking revenge by trying to cause undue pain, mutilate, or even torture someone?" Imagine yourself or your lawyer trying to explain away that kind of inquisition. Even anti-gun folks know the reputation of the shotgun, and even if that reputation is full of Hollywood inaccuracies, you will be in a bad way on the witness stand. Stay conventional.

The last advantage I'll mention should be obvious to everyone, but just in case, know that a quality, combat-ready shotgun is priced far lower than nearly any brand new AR. This is regardless of make.

Now for the downside. While I said before that one of the riot gun's greatest assets was its effectiveness at short range (under 25 yards), it's that same range that is also it's biggest disadvantage. The one small exception to this is with the use of sabot rounds (which contain a sub-caliber projectile housed in a sabot, or plastic "shoe"), which can extend the shotgun's effective range, due to

The riot shotgun is not for everyone, due to recoil. If mounted to the shoulder properly, as demonstrated by this state trooper, recoil isn't a problem. Note the foot position and how he leans into instead of away from the gun. Recoil can be further mitigated through the use of reduced-recoil shot and slugs in pump shotguns. Twenty-gauge riot guns, such as those available through Ithaca, are also a worthy consideration.

their higher velocity when compared to bore-diameter rifled slugs. This advantage is small. Sabot's still require a rifled barrel to shoot to their accuracy and distance potential, and a rifled barrel ruins the versatility of the shotgun, as it inhibits the patterning of shot rounds compared to the same run through a smoothbore.

Let's talk about some other forms of ammo and their limitations. Out of smoothbore riot gun barrels, buckshot runs out of serious steam around 40 yards. Accuracy potential from rifled slugs is limited to not much past 100 yards. This keeps the shotgun limited in use against longer-range threats and defines why a shotgun alone should not be the only firearm in your survival armory.

The next most significant weakness of the standard shotgun is the magazine capacity. Riot gun capacity is generally limited to a maximum of eight rounds or less in the magazine tube, unless you attach some huge competition magazine system. That's fine, but such add-ons hamper the portability of the weapon and can make the firearm unwieldy. The exception to this issue might be the 14-round Kel-Tec KSG pump. A bullpup design with twin under-barrel magazine tubes, the KSF is extremely compact. It is also a brand new design, not one adapted from sporting weapons, such as are nearly every one of today's tactical shotguns. It may provide the solution to the limited capacity issue. I've never handled or fired one, but reviews seem to be favorable. What I don't know about is the long-term endurance of this weapon under hard use. Until there is proof of its durability, I'd stick with a conventional tactical pump with an eight-round magazine—and eight at the very most, as six is really more ideal—and practice your loading/reloading technique until you have it down to a smooth, nearly automatic drill. Also add in training drills where you transition from an empty shotgun to a high-capacity pistol or other weapon until you can get your shotgun reloaded. You will need a sling for your weapon to accomplish this technique successfully; you don't want to drop it while you're working with another firearm.

Top Shotgun Picks

There are a lot of very good to excellent tactical shotguns that make good riot guns, and I worked with a large number of the best for my Tactical Shotgun book. I won't rehash all the choices that are possible here, since not all of them are at their best for riot gun-type duty. Instead I will give you my top three personal picks for survival shotguns. Note that none of them have pistol grips, which I feel reduce pointability and slow deployment.

First up is the Ithaca Model 37 Defense Gun in either the four- or eight-shot model and with the genuine walnut stock. Walnut has been used successfully far longer than synthetics for military rifle stocks, and its durability is well tested. These Model 37s I am talking about are *real* Ithacas (not a foreign-made knock-off), one manufactured in Upper Sandusky, Ohio, on CNC machinery and with hand craftsmanship at a very reasonable price. The Model 37 was the favorite of the LAPD and NYPD, to name a few. Its solid-frame design allows only one entry point for dirt, as well as for loading and unloading of shells. The one I have is equipped with the simplest, or "riot," gun sight, that being a single brass bead. Marbles brand adjustable sights with light gathering tubes are available, as well. While the bead is quite visible in low light, simple to use, quick to acquire, and nearly indestructible, it won't give you the long-range precision with slugs that you might want.

The 12-gauge version of the Model 37 weighs in at a very light seven pounds, while the 20-gauge weighs in at 6.5. The Defense shotgun is coated in a protective matte coating that has a slight greenish caste. As such it is very well camouflaged in rural and urban settings. When I tested it with some members of my former sheriff's office, who were accustomed to Remington 870s—*the* standard in police and sporting pump shotguns—with full pistol-grip stocks, they loved the light weight and pointability. Overall, this is an affordable, battle-proven (in both military and law enforcement street combat), classic that will serve you well.

Next up is the Mossberg 590A1 with an M4 collapsible stock. The A1 is the military-issue version of the storied Mossberg 500 and has only recently been made available to the civilian public. This shotgun worked out for me better than any other I tested for my *Tactical Shotgun* book. If I was going strictly on ergonomics alone, this would be my No. 1 pick.

While the 590A1 is available in several variations, the one with the collapsible M4 stock works best for me. I suffer from a deterioration of mobility in my shoulders, the result of teaching police defensive tactics for some 20-plus years. The damage has caused me to lose a great deal of normal flexibility, which translates into me having difficulty handling rifles and shotguns whose length of pull (the distance from the butt to the receiver) is on the long side. It seems like there are a lot of shotguns out there that way, but this isn't one of them.

I shoot all my M4-stocked guns, rifles and shotguns, as I learned to from my combat-hardened friends in the Army Special Forces (specifically the Green Berets), with the stock all the way closed, body armor or no body armor. My nose is close to touching the charging handle on the left side. (Okay, in a rifle, for a caliber heavier than 5.56, I use a little more extension to avoid getting smacked in the face). I keep the Mossberg locked down like that, and because of that, it is very quick to the target for me.

One of the other cool things about the M4 stock is that the stock is not in a direct line with the barrel. It actually slopes down from the receiver. This has the effect of mitigating felt recoil. Also, because the stock can be collapsed down, the 5901A1 would be a great shotgun to travel with—and if you really want to shorten it for low-profile transportation, dismount the barrel.

Beyond the personal ergonomics, the 590A1 is rock solid, with Mil-Spec reliability. My version has non-adjustable rifle sights (actually, they're more like pistol sights, three-dot, in fact), which shoot dead on and are impossible to mess up. According to the Mossberg online catalog, the company is no longer offering these sights, the choices now being between bead and ghost ring peep sights.

The 590A1 is available with five-plus-one or eight-plus-one magazine capacities. Mine is the five-shot magazine, which also features Mossberg's ambidextrous tang-mounted safety. While I am more used to the pushbutton safeties of the Remington 870, Ithaca 37, and M1 Carbine, I like the Mossberg design, not so much because it's ambidextrous, but because I can see that it's on or off every time I mount the gun to my face; no rolling it to the side to double-check as with other models (yeah, I know, you can feel it, but you need to visually check it, as well).

The 590A1 is very smooth in operation for a tactical shotgun in its price range (around $500), and has become more popular than once was the Remington 870. The 590A1 is an excellent tactical and riot shotgun.

My last pick for a pump is the Remington 887 Nitro Mag Tactical. It is the very best in pump shotguns Remington has to offer. The Remington 870, of course, is still very alive and well and is a great shotgun, with variations available for every purpose, but

The Remington 887 is the top tier in out-of-the-box-ready tactical shotguns. Length of pull and price are just right. This is not a reworked 870, but is, rather, twenty-first century new. Coupled with Remington's Managed Recoil buckshot or slugs (the civilian version of the popular law enforcement reduced recoil load), the 887 stands ready to meet your CQB or mid-range needs.

it is not without its faults. Even with its anti-jam feed tab update, the 870 still can lock up from time to time and require emergency field clearing. While the ergonomics are okay, they are only that. I have never picked up any variation of the 870 and gasped, "I *gotta* have me one of these!" So, while the 870 is a durable, fairly reliable workhorse (remember, it was the 590A1 that made the military Mil-Spec-grade approval), there is a better Remington pump-action now, one for the twenty-first century.

While it operates with controls similar to the 870's, the 887 is not simply a dressed up, worked-over version of that revered model. It is, rather, a new design. Extremely capable out of the box

and with all the tactical features the average shooter could want, including a tactical muzzle break and a $450 price tag, the 887 Nitro Mag Tactical is one of the few fixed-stock shotguns that has fit me without modification. Additionally, the Armor LOKT protective polymer finish makes it nearly impervious to the elements or hard knocks. You could throw this baby in the bed of a pickup truck or the toolbox and not have to worry about it getting torn up. It was a standout when I tested it for my book *Tactical Shotguns*, since all the rails for optics and lights were already in place. (And no, just because it has rails for optics and lights, it doesn't mean you have to mount them.) You simply cannot beat a deal like this.

A formidable woman with a formidable firearm—in this case a Wilson Combat shotgun—is more than capable of defending her area of responsibility from a takeover.

The shotgun can still dominate as a CQB-type of weapon for defense against single or multiple aggressors, whether they are of the two- or four-legged variety.

The shotgun still sees some action with S.W.A.T. teams. In this case, the shotgun is the Benelli M1 semi-automatic. While many S.W.A.T. teams favor semi-autos, the pump-action models are the best survival guns, because they can fire any type of 12- gauge load without balking. The recoil-operated Benellis are great guns, but may not function reliably with reduced-recoil loads.

Chapter 7

HANDGUNS: DON'T LEAVE HOME WITHOUT ONE

A handgun (or several) is essential to your civil disorder survival gear. You simply can't get by without them. Handguns are the final firearms used during close-quarter battle situations, or one may also be the only firearm you have with you when the balloon goes up. Obviously, you won't be packing an AR in a movie theater, only the evil do that. With some forethought, you are going to be using a handgun, and hopefully it is big enough to do the job.

But the handgun is not only for CQB situations. With the right handgun and the right practice, you can effectively hit human-size targets out to 200 yards, free standing and with no optic attached. The fact that you can be effective at extended distances is important to understand and a skill you should be able to perform. With Ohio changing its minimum police qualifications from a 60-round course to

While the 1911 .45 ACP (mounted on the armor in the background) is a superior pistol shot for shot over a 9mm weapon, at only 7+1 rounds it lacks the magazine capacity of the 15+1 Beretta 92/M9 military pistol. The most recent M9 variant is the M9A1 with a built-in front rail, shown in the foreground with the BLACKHAWK! Xiphos tactical light attached. The grips are Crimson Trace's Lasergrips and the sights are XS Sights small dot express sights with a tritium front insert. While the tactical light and laser sight are an excellent addition to the M9A1 for tactical law enforcement use, they aren't needed on a dedicated survival handgun.

a 25-round course and had its officers and trainees firing just two rounds at 50 feet shows a lack of understanding for the need of long-distance handgun fight tactics. This new "standard" does a great disservice to the officers in Ohio, in terms of their ability to defend themselves and also to the people they are sworn to defend. To make matters worse, officers can fail the 50-foot portion of the course, and as long as they pass the other reduced-distance portions, they are deemed to have qualified.

Small-town PDs previously required by law to shoot the 60-round course each year will jump for administrative joy at the savings in ammo and overtime. (Oh, and don't worry about shooting after dark, as officers no longer have to do that, either). But what does this say about their view of the world? While the states claim departments can do all the extra training they want, which is true, they are ignoring the long-term realities of the economic depression—yep, that's what I said—we are currently being suffocated by.

Anyone out there think they don't need long-distance handgun competency? Listen to this.

I have a friend, Brandon Moore, who was a deputy at the nearby Morrow County Sheriff's Office. He was ambushed by a marijuana grower who began shooting him with a 5.56mm AR-15 from around 70 yards. Brandon, working plainclothes but wearing soft body armor and carrying a full-size Smith & Wesson M&P .40 with two spare magazines, was shot through the thigh and scrotum. The AR rounds blew out part of his testicles, then passed through the left leg, blowing away a chunk of tibia and causing that leg to be permanently shorter than the right. A final round from the pot grower penetrated the armor, slowing down, but taking out his spleen and collapsing a lung before its travel stopped.

Severely wounded, Brandon couldn't make it back into his car to retrieve his AR, so he went to war with his M&P. In a rollover prone position with the gun in his right hand, and while clutching his scrotum with his left, Brandon returned fire, with multiple rounds and reloads, from a laser-measured distance of 64 yards, across a span of time that went at least 10 minutes.

I was guarding Moore's assailant when the doctor came in to deliver the news of the guy's condition. Brandon's .40-caliber rounds had struck the shooter twice in the soft armor he was wearing, causing severe bruising, while the rest of the rounds had shattered the man's right heel and totally pulverized eight inches of tibial bone in the same leg. His right foot was being held to the rest of his leg by some remaining flesh and a stainless steel rod. The assailant was forbidden to put any weight on his right foot until the doctors could figure out what they were going to do to permanently fix it; the rod was merely keeping the foot from flopping around. Whatever they figured out, the shooter was destined to be indisposed for a long time. Brandon, one of the most courageous men I have ever met, required multiple surgeries but returned to the job before eventually retiring.

Recently, I taught an extended-range handgun class, with shots fired out to 100 yards, with Brandon's assistance. The class, Brandon included, fired the "Brandon Moore Drill" from the same distance as had been measured in the actual firefight, and in the same position, including holding their crotches. Brandon beat everyone and agreed that it was much easier to do when you aren't bleeding out. In any event, the lesson here is that the handgun can be effective at long range is one important to understand, and being capable with a handgun at extended distances is a skill set you should be ready to use should the need arise.

Handguns for survival use in societal disorder situations have the same basic requirements that rifles and shotguns do. The characteristics of reliability, ruggedness, portability, simplicity, effectiveness, and sustainability are just as critical. Now, portability may seem to be an "oh, duh" type of requirement for a handgun, since they are designed to be portable, but it really isn't. For example, if you don't expect your travels to carry you through wilderness areas where grizzly bears roam, than a handgun chambered in .500 Smith & Wesson or even "just" a .44 Magnum simply isn't required and, in fact, can be detrimental. Portability for a handgun also doesn't mean you have to have a primary handgun as small as the Ruger LCP. What you need is a standard size, standard make, law enforcement or military duty sidearm, *in its most basic configuration*, meaning lights, optics, or custom competition modifications of any kind are not only *not* needed, but *detrimental* to the mission. Also, it should be a high-capacity weapon—remember the concept of *crowd* control—of a commonly available caliber.

There are six basic centerfire calibers to consider (rimfires will be examined later), and I will list them in order of preference. They are the 9mm, .40 Smith & Wesson, .45 ACP, .357 Magnum, .38 Special (I know, these last two are for revolvers) and, just to stir things up a bit, the 5.7x28mm. While I love the .357 SIG and .38 Super and would take them over the .40 in a gunfight (the .357 SIG was our duty caliber at the Sheriff's office), they are not easily obtainable calibers. Again, these are my personal favorites, but I need to provide you with the guns and calibers that are best for survival.

Semi-Autos—Your First Choice

In the world of pistols, there are quite a few that will work well for survival, so don't be offended if I don't list your favorite pistol. If it meets the six requirements and you like and can afford it, then it will serve you. But back to my choices. The semi-automatic pistol that I would choose above all the others out there in 9mm is the Beretta 92 (military designation M9), or the updated 92A1 (military designation M9A1), now available to civilians and which includes a light rail. I only mention the A1 as a choice because, if you already have one that works, but don't buy another for the rail because a weapons light isn't necessary. It also costs you $40 more than the standard-frame version. Also, there are not as many holsters available as of this

The pistol is ideal for CQB, particularly when one needs a hand available to complete another task besides defense. Here, one survivor covers with a pistol as this door is pried open, after which the defender on the right can grab the handle of the door to pull it open for his partner while tucking the pistol in close to his body for protection. The pistol is the Beretta 92 (M9).

writing for the A1, as it was a late arrival to the civilian field. The tricked up 90-Two model, sorta the polymer-framed, Italian sports car version of the 92, also works if you have it already, but it's $50 more than that the 92FS. While the Beretta 92 is also available as the .40-caliber model 96, it would be wise to avoid it, since it is not widely distributed, thereby limiting replacement magazine availability. (Holsters aren't a problem for it, as anything that works for the 92 works for the 96).

There are plenty of 9mm naysayers out there, and there is some validity to their concerns. However, there are a lot of positive things going for the round, including lower cost, lower recoil, lower muzzle blast and flash, lighter weight, and universal availability. I, for one, am totally comfortable with the 9mm and use it as my duty caliber. There are also plenty of documented failures out there with the .40 S&W in law enforcement shootings, especially in the 180-grain bullet weight. In essence, it is not the "magic bullet" it was originally hoped to be. But more on that later.

As far as the 92 goes, there is no questioning the reliability of the original Beretta 92FS/M9. It has been given the ultimate field test, since 1985, as the U.S. Armed Force's standard-issue battle pistol. Used in all types of environments, it has passed with flying colors. With a legendary smoothness of operation rivaled only by custom pistols, (the slide runs like it's on ball bearings), the 92 was, for much of the 1980s and into the '90s, second only to Smith & Wesson in terms of police service use. That changed with the advent of the Glock safe-action trigger design and its acceptance as being simpler and easier to operate than the high-capacity double-action/single-action 9mm of any other make and model.

As far as the 92 series goes, it just runs and runs and runs. In one of the Army trials, 12 Beretta M9s fired a total of 168,000 rounds without a single malfunction. I have never had a malfunction on my personal 92FS, and the only ones I have observed were when the shooter tried to substitute aftermarket magazines for Beretta factory originals. I am not sure why this is, but don't take the chance. Spend a bit more for the real McCoy.

In terms of ruggedness, the same qualities that make the 92 reliable also bolster its ruggedness. Its design has stood up to the worst environmental conditions on earth and the worst neglect possible by men in combat. It is still going strong some 27 years after its adoption, even though potential replacements have been examined in the recent past. True, the SIG has supplanted the Beretta in certain situations, such as for use by the Navy SEALs, and has also been ad-

A closeup of the tried and true Beretta Model 92, showing its double-action/single-action trigger and ambidextrous safety system.

opted by the Coast Guard recently, but the M9 and M9A1 remain the military standard. The only other duty handgun to survive in service that long was, of course, the .45 ACP Model 1911.

Portability is less of an issue when discussing protective handguns than it is when talking long guns. While the 92 may not be the best choice for deep cover carry under current conditions, it still can be done. I know, because I've done it. There are many ways to carry the 92 out of plain sight—backpack, sling pack, fanny pack, IWB holster carry, or belt carry with specialized holsters like the innovative types from Crossbreed.

I earlier mentioned simplicity of operation as a requirement. This is an area where the 92 gives up some ground to a few more modern designs such as the Glock. (However, the 92 doesn't give up ground on its metal magazine versus Glock's plastic. I replace broken Glock 19 magazines on our academy guns. The plastic ends up breaking off the body of the magazine tube body in the area forward of the follower.) As I'll expand on in the sidebar "DA/SA or One Action Only?" the 92 has a manual safety/decocker and the standard DA/SA trigger requires transition practice. Some find this to be a problem. I haven't, since the first duty autos I carried in my law enforcement career were the early Smith & Wesson series, starting with the elegant Model 39. Training and practice will overcome any such issue.

Finally we come to effectiveness. No, the 9mm in FMJ bullet profile is not as effective as the FMJ .45 as it relates to raw potential for stopping a determined assailant. However, there are many more 9mm rounds available to you, 15 per mag rather than seven or eight in a single-stack .45. Get proper hits with all those 9mm bullets and you will be effective. If I am anticipating the need for close-range protection from large amounts of people, I want to put as much ammo downrange as possible, and the high capacity of a 9mm will allow me to do just that. Taking all that into consideration, the Beretta 92FS is simply an excellent delivery system.

Okay, before everyone starts firing up the hate mail, I'll go ahead and list several others that will meet the parameters and serve as effective sidearms in time of civil collapse. While the Beretta 92 once held the military market as well as a sizeable chunk of the civilian and law enforcement side, with the LAPD once being renowned for carrying this gun, it has been overshadowed and replaced by newer, more modern, striker-fired pistols. And I will say that having a copy of the very same gun used by the law enforcement officers in your area is a wise idea, unless the gun is in a less than commonly available caliber, such as .357 SIG (I wish this round had come out before the .40 Smith & Wesson, rather than formed from it and introduced after). Same with the nearly non-existent .45 GAP (Glock Auto Pistol), which, while adopted by a couple moderate-sized agencies, was doomed to failure from the start.

While the original concept was to fit the .45 GAP into a pistol exactly the same size as the Glock 17 and 23, things just didn't work out that way. The .45 GAP is simply a short .45 ACP (at least on the surface), which initially allowed bullets up to 200 grains in weight. As its development progressed, technicians found a way to make 230-grain bullets work in it. While the round fit the frame, it didn't fit the slide, so nothing of existing dimensions worked. The barrel and slide assembly had to be enlarged to fit the new cartridge and its operating pressures. The full-size .45 ACP frame and slide were unnecessarily and undesirably large, and the Glock 17 frame and slide were too small. In the end, the .45 GAP failed to become the .45-caliber Glock pistol that would fit any existing holster for a Glock 17, its original intent, and, well, nobody bought it.

With that being said, there are a still a lot of Glocks to choose

The Glock is the most common law enforcement duty pistol in America, residing in somewhere around 70 percent of all police holsters. Here, this woman's DPMS AP4 carbine is backed up by a Second Generation Glock 17 riding securely in a BLACKHAWK! Serpa holster.

from in 9mm, .40 S&W, and .45 ACP. With anywhere from 67 to 70 percent of all law enforcement officers in the United States using some variation of the Glock, it becomes an easily supportable weapon. Since we are sticking with duty-size pistols, the mini-Glocks, the ultimate concealment versions, are out. That leaves you with the choice of mid-range pistols such as the Model 19 in 9mm, Model 23 in .40, the Model 30 in .45 ACP, and the full-size pistols in the same respective chambering's, the Models 17, 22, and 21. Glock is currently producing its Generation 4 variants, which have improvements, the most important being the ability to adjust the size of the grip for small, medium, and large hands. However, you don't need a Gen 4 pistol to do the job if you find a good used older version.

That being said, there are two Glock variations you should avoid. The first are the short-lived Generation 3s. They feature an overly aggressive checkering design molded into the frame. The idea was to provide a better grip surface for officers who wear tactical gloves in the line of duty. What was discovered in very short order, though, was that the checkering was so intense it hurt to shoot the gun for very long with un-gloved hands. Officer uniforms were also getting torn to shreds from contact with the grips. The Gen 3s had the checkering dialed down when they became the Generation 4s.

The other used Glock pistols you want to avoid are the first-generation .40-caliber versions with the non-upgraded frame. The very first Glock, the Model 17, was designed for the 9mm caliber. When the .40 S&W round hit the scene, Glock saw a good thing and found that it could, unlike the .45 GAP, fit the .40 right into that 9mm envelope. A problem that arose shortly thereafter, and one that was easily solved, had to do with the higher pressure levels of the .40 over the 9mm.

In this case, the pistol's locking block, which is what basically holds the slide to the frame during discharge, started shearing off after a fair amount of shooting. The fix was to add a locking block pin to the locking block right above the trigger pin on the frame. Soon thereafter, all Glocks, including all the 9mms, added the locking block pin to the frame as standard equipment, thus making manufacture consistent and reducing liability.

I have a Glock 17 I've fired for many thousands of rounds with the original frame and no locking block pin, as well as a number of Glock 19s also with the original frame and that have been in service for much higher round counts, and have never had a problem with them. Just don't get a used one in .40 without the extra pin, unless Glock will upgrade the frame for you at no charge.

One final thing about the Glock series of pistols. Any of the mid-size pistols will fit in leather for the full-size versions, but not necessarily vice-versa, and any of the mid-size guns (and for that manner the minis), will accept any magazine from the larger models of the same caliber.

Another popular choice for a police duty pistol, maybe the second most popular, at least in my region, are the Smith & Wesson M&P (Military and Police) high-capacity pistols available in 9mm, .40 S&W, and .45 ACP. When Smith & Wesson introduced its DA/SA Model 39, it was on the way to dominating, at least for awhile, the semi-automatic police duty pistol market through its own three generations of pistols that followed that original Model 39. If you are unsure what generation a used Smith & Wesson DA/SA autoloader is, just check the number of digits in the model name. For instance two numbers (the 39 and, later, the high-cap 59) indicate the first generation pistols, which didn't work well with many 9mm hollowpoint designs then on the market. The Model 39 is the best feeling pistol in my hand I ever owned or shot, but I wouldn't pick up a used one at this point in time for any reason. For one, it uses eight-shot magazines, and those magazines are no longer readily available. Nor are some of the parts. Likewise, for survival purposes, I'd decline the Model 59. This was a 15-shot version of the 39 and the first high-capacity 9mm to hit the market. However, it suffered some of the reliability shortcomings the 39 did, maybe more.

Three digits in the S&W model number, such as will be the 559 or 659 9mms, are the much improved second generation pistols. This generation also included the Model 645, an eight-shot, all-stainless, double-action .45 ACP that was big, reliable, and did away with the cocked-and-locked carry concerns of police administrators when officers wanted to carry, but were denied, single-action 1911 Colt .45s. The 645 took the police world by storm. It was the first duty autoloader reliable enough to be adopted by the Reynoldsburg PD while I worked there full time, and the second autoloader approved for the Union County Sheriff's Office, where I worked for 20 years as a reserve. It was also the first duty autoloader adopted by the city of Columbus' 1,400-man force. Indeed, Smith & Wesson began pushing the 9mm Beretta out of the police market with this gun. Smith then introduced some refinements to its second generation pistols and brought out the third generation, which used four digits in its model designations. The 645 became the 4506 and gathered even more acceptance in police holsters. Both .45-caliber pistol generations are often found on the used gun market.

The GSG 1911 comes with a good set of high-visibility combat/target sights.

And then came Glock, and manufacturer fortunes changed again. Glock took Smith & Wesson's new .40-caliber round and ran with it, leaving Smith in the dust for quite a few years, as departments turned in their DA/SA pistols wholesale for the new Glock.

Smith tried to counter the success with a Glock-like variant known as the Sigma. Patterned after the Glock design to the point that Glock sued Smith (unsuccessfully), the Sigma is basically a good pistol, and inexpensive compared to the Glock, but it isn't the equal, due mostly to the Smith & Wesson version of a "Safe-Action" trigger system that produces a substandard trigger pull. Adoption of Sigmas was spotty, at best.

Don't confuse the Sigma with the M&P pistol. They are different guns, though they look somewhat similar on the exterior and both have a good ergonomic feel. I would rate the Sigma pistol as a good value for civilian home-defense in normal times, but that is about it.

Finally, Smith came out with the M&P autoloaders, a much more advanced and capable pistol than the Sigma in terms of trigger pull, adaptability (it was one of the first to use an adjustable grip system), and quality. It was adopted by the Columbus PD to replace their aging and now out-of-production 4506s. From having worked with CPD in various capacities over the years, I can tell you two reasons that force went with the M&P over the Glock. The first was a deep-seated and long-term relationship with Smith & Wesson, and the second is the fact that the M&P can be field stripped without having to pull the trigger, a requirement with the Glock system.

The M&P, in my book, had one other factor in its favor over the Glock, and that is generally better ergonomics, even beyond the adaptability of the grip size to the individual user. It just feels better in the hand than the Glock, and I say that viewed against the adjust-able-grip Generation 4 Glocks.

There were a couple minor glitches with the M&P that would have been hard to discover without many agencies putting it into service, just as there are with any new gun. The M&P, like the Glock, is available in three sizes in each caliber. There is also an optional and additional manual safety available on certain models, unlike the Glock. If I was looking to purchase a survival pistol and was trying to decide between the two, I would base my decision upon which felt better in my hand or which was cheaper, depending on which factor was more personally important to you.

The last potential choice in survival autoloading pistols for me would be any model made by SIG Sauer. Let me say that SIG builds excellent handguns based on its original DA/SA designs from the 1970s. There are a large number of variants, including frames available in steel, aluminum, or polymer, and operating systems that begin with the original DA/SA models and add single-action, double-action, or DAK (Double Action Kellerman, named after its inventor), advanced trigger systems.

As mentioned, the SIG in the form of the 9mm 229, has had some limited military adoption and has graced the duty holsters of a few, but not many, police officers. There has been only one reason for this lack of enthusiasm by law enforcement for this brand, and that is cost. SIGs can run $200 or more per duty gun when compared to Glocks, M&Ps, or Berettas, and that's a deal breaker, especially when you're talking about a firearm that offers no technical advantage over others against which it is compared. While most of the DA/SAs that SIG has offered use the decock-only system (no safety—again, see this chapter's sidebar), that doesn't explain the lack of popularity, especially considering that SIG Sauers really are excellent guns. That leaves cost, and that differential used to be even higher when all of SIG Sauer guns were made in Germany. If you have a SIG pistol in a common caliber (at one time SIGs were available in .38 Super, and were used by the Secret Service), or you want to buy one because you like it, then it works for me. But don't feel like that is your must-have gun just because of a recommendation by a gun counter sales clerk.

Revolvers—Second but Sound Choices

Yes, I realize that I missed at least two other major auto-loading gun manufacturers, and that I skipped the 1911 pistols all together, but trust me readers, and take it from someone who, as a cop, has been surrounded by large, angry crowds on at least three occasions during his career: there just aren't enough bullets available in most 1911s to fend off a crowd for very long. I would rather be causing a number of "Gee, maybe I shouldn't have started bothering this particular group of people" injuries than fewer but more serious wounds. This statement may seem a bit odd, as it precedes a discussion of a limited capacity defensive weapon, the revolver.

While the capacity of the revolver is limited to a maximum of eight in production revolvers of .38 Special/.357 Magnum caliber or larger, the average revolver is going to have a capacity of six rounds (five for the smallest frame snubnose revolvers). Despite the low supply of rounds aboard, the revolver has a couple important things going for it.

First, the design is very reliable as long as it is kept reasonably clean. Second, it is not dependent on magazines to keep it operational, so there are none to drop out or leave behind. Third, it is probably the fastest handgun into action compared to any other type. No safety is involved, and once the weapon is loaded, it's ready to rock. Action type should be double-action (not the Old West-style single-action revolver), with a chambering of .357 Magnum caliber as the most

A small revolver (such as this S&W Model 642), backed up by a light and spare ammo, is an excellent off-duty weapon for law enforcement officers. Today it is the starting point in off-duty armament. It should be backed by a full-size revolver or pistol, as well as a rifle such as the AR-15.

versatile of choices, since a revolver chambered for .357 can also chamber the shorter .38 Special or even the rarer .38 Long Colt and .38 Short Colt rounds.

The .357 and .38 are probably the most widely distributed pistol ammunition of any type, and if your long gun happens to be an 1894C Marlin or something similar, your ammo load is simplified. In fact, it would be good to have a .357 revolver on hand, just so you have something that could shoot this readily available ammo.

What make and model? There is no more solid or reliable .357 Magnum revolver than the Ruger GP100 series. While I still bear some unresolved anger at Ruger for ever having gotten rid of its smaller frame Security and Speed Six series (which were the very best of the type), in favor of the GP100, I am over it enough to recommend the GP100 as my top choice. The smaller S&W K-frame-sized Security Six (adjustable sight) and Speed Six (fixed sight) found their way into many police holsters in the 1980s. If you have one, hang onto it, for it, too, shares the same level of indestructibility as the GP100s. I have never seen or heard of one going out of time as I've seen with Colt's and Smith & Wesson revolvers, although I am sure there are one or two.

The other factor that makes these Ruger revolvers my survival choice is that they can be field stripped darn near like a semi-auto pistol for maintenance. Springs and other parts can be changed by the average person, even by me, and I'm often a menace with tools in my hands. I even changed out the standard spring set in the Security Six for a Wolff set for a smoother trigger pull without messing anything up. While Smith & Wesson revolvers may seem a bit more refined, in part because the company still produces a large line (the majority in the snubby J-frame size), I would go with the GP100, and even though Smith has some seven- and eight-shot models in its larger L-frame series. The field strip benefit of the Rugers is just too crucially important for long-term operation, particularly if your gun would get dropped in mud or some other unfriendly substance. I won't likely gear up with one because I still have the classic Model 67 Combat Masterpiece in .38 Special I carried on duty at the start of my law enforcement career. If you are in a similar situation, you can do the same, but if you don't have a .38 or, better yet, a .357, try to add a four-inch Ruger GP100 to your survival collection and stock up on .38 Special ammo. If you run across .357 ammo, that's fine, but it's a lot harder to shoot, even in a handgun this large. Get speedloaders for it, practice loading with them, and get a comfortable belt-mounted holster for it.

DA/SA or One Action Only?

A quick definition of double-action/single-action (DA/SA) semi-auto pistols is prudent here. First seen on the Walther PPK and P38, and later on the Smith & Wesson Models 39 and 59, the term simply means that, from the de-cocked safety-off position, the trigger will both cock and release the hammer. Trigger pull in the DA mode will weigh about 12 pounds. Subsequent shots will be in the single-action mode, whereby all the trigger does is release the hammer. Trigger pull is usually reduced to about five pounds in this mode. Once the firing string is done, in pistols with de-cocking levers like the Beretta, the de-cocking lever is pushed and the hammer is safely dropped down into the original de-cocked position, and the pistol is ready to fire in the DA mode again.

This system is often criticized as being difficult to train with due to making the transition from the 12-pound DA pull to the five-pound SA pull on the second shot. I don't believe it is. The very first centerfire pistol I owned was the DA/SA Smith & Wesson Model 39. Following that, I carried for many years a Walther PPK/S in .380 ACP as my duty pistol on the narcotics unit and as an off-duty gun while working uniform patrol. What the DA first shot provides, due to the heavy 12-pound trigger pull, is the reduction in a first shot accidental discharge in real life situations where adrenalin is high, usually even if the shooter's finger is on the trigger (just like in the days when the revolver ruled). Our current necessary and stringent admonition to our cops and recruits is to keep the trigger finger 'on frame" until ready to actually shoot. This lesson didn't become as necessary until the massive acceptance by law enforcement of the Glock with its standard 5.5-pound trigger pull; I guarantee there are far fewer accidental shots fired in stress by law enforcement officers armed with the 92.

There is one caveat to that statement, and that is you must train, train, and train to *decock* the DA/SA pistol after any string of fire and before re-holstering your weapon (just like you must train to *apply the safety* on the 1911 before holstering), or there will likely be a discharge into the ground or your foot at some time. As long as you train with the decocker, you are golden. Be advised, there are a number of variations on this theme. For most Berettas, the decocker is also a safety. When you push down the lever, the pistol will decock, the lever will stay down in the safe position, and the pistol will not fire unless you push the lever back up to the fire position. I like this format, because you can put the safety in the on or down position when you charge the weapon (chamber a round). When you do that, the hammer will already be down (decocked) as a result of racking the slide and all you have to do is push the lever up to be ready to fire in the double-action mode.

This type of safety-on decock lever is also featured on the Walther PP/PPK, but SIG DA/SA pistols, which are also an excellent survival pistol choice but more expensive than the Beretta and others, use a lever that functions only as a de-cocker and not as an additional safety. Pistols based on the CZ-75, on the other hand, will have only a safety lever, similar in operation to that of a single-action-only 1911 pistol. There is no safe form of a de-cocker, other than your thumb firmly on the hammer to prevent its rapid fall forward, a gentle trigger finger, and the muzzle pointed in a safe direction. These pistols can be carried like the Browning Hi Power, cocked and locked, and perform with single-action trigger operation for the fist and subsequent shots and, if you've safely dropped the hammer manually after chambering around, will also fire in double-action mode for the first shot. Just remember there is no grip safety like you'll find on a 1991 that is used as a backup to the thumb safety on these guns, so be careful.

Chapter 8

LESS LETHAL, STILL NECESSARY

"Guns don't survive, people do."

A firearm is only one part—a *very* important part—but only one part of your survival plan, and they need to be supported or supplemented by other weapons and options. I addressed the bayonet as one of those options, and it's a darn good one, but there are others to be considered.

Not everyone will have access to a long gun that can mount a bayonet, but everyone needs a fixed-blade knife. Folders are out the window at this point, unless that's all you have. They simply will not stand up to the tasks they will be asked to perform, like emergency digging and prying, not to mention fighting. Only a fixed blade can do those things. But which ones?

Like firearms, the high-quality middle ground is what I'm looking for in a fixed blade. I don't have an unlimited budget and I can do everything with a mid-range priced fixed blade that I can with a high priced custom or semi-custom blade, marketing claims to the contrary.

While it's possible to get some Chinese-made products that are of reasonable quality, I certainly prefer something that is American made, or at least made in a country that has truly been an ally of the United States. For example, Smith & Wesson-brand knives are produced for that company by Taylor brands and manufactured in the U.S. They are of fine quality and very reasonably priced. You can often find them on sale in the mid-$20 price range. For example, the S&W "Search and Rescue" fixed-blade knife is on sale as I write this on Amazon.com for $24.83. I originally paid $35 for this model three years ago, and I still think that was a fair price. Modeled after the Ka-Bar fighting knives with a black-coated blade, standard edge, and rubber handle, it comes with a nylon/plastic sheath with a leg tie-down strap and a compartment for a sharpening stone. The pommel is flat and can be used for pounding. I originally used this knife for S.W.A.T. duties, but then kept it in my patrol kit while working the road. Obviously, it would be a first choice for survival duties if a bayonet were not available.

Smith & Wesson knives are produced in an almost "knife of the week club" format, with new models in my area gun shop showing up nearly every seven days. If you see one in a dealer's case or online that you like, you might want to pick it up quick, as some models seem to become discontinued quickly.

I have a S&W tactical folder with a window breaking tip on one end. It is an assisted-opening model with a safety lock and opens in the blink of an eye. But I've noticed over time that, while being carried in a pocket with things such as car keys, the tan finish on the scales has started to wear off. This truly is cosmetic only, so no big deal. I would rather have the nice finish wear a little rather than have the knife break, and certainly would choose to save the money over something with more durable cosmetics.

Speaking of Ka-Bar, its fighting knives are still quite available, and most products, such as the military blades, are U.S.-made. It does, however, import some knives under its brand name that are made to the company's specifications in China. If you found a model you liked that was made in China under the Ka-Bar brand or other known maker's brand, then go ahead and buy it. Ka-Bar and others wouldn't allow their name on it if it was junk, it would hurt their entire lines.

Buck is operating in a similar fashion these days, with some of its knives made in the USA and some off-shore. It's easy to discern which is which simply by the difference in price—most of the off-shore stuff is in the mid-$20 price range—and also by the fact that the USA-made knives are marked with an American flag next to the lifetime warranty marking (which all Buck knives have).

Your fixed-blade knife should be one marked "tactical" or specifically designed as a fighting blade. But, if you have a Buck Pathfinder hunting knife, for example, don't feel like you need to trade it off for another brand, like Ka-Bar. The Pathfinder, as its name implies, will serve you well, since most combat knives have hunting or outdoors blades as part of their heritage. While the pommel of the Pathfinder isn't designed for pounding, the rest of the knife will do everything one of the fighting blades will do.

Columbia River Knife and Tool has a huge line of knives of mostly overseas manufacture. CRKT has consulted with a number of custom knife makers in the design of its knives and has come up with some of the most innovative blades and tools available. Some of the fixed-blade survival knives, including the fine MAK-1 Rescue tool that I did a bit of consulting on, have a flat, chisel-style point designed for prying. While I prefer a pointed tip on a survival knife, since there is a possibility it will be used for a stabbing thrust, a chisel prying tip can come in handy when it comes to foraging for food, and the carbide pointed tip makes short work of breaking window glass found on vehicle side windows without endangering the person doing the breaking. The MAK-1 was the official fixed-blade knife for our 727 Counter Terror Training Unit when it was in operation.

Ontario Knives are made in the USA and come in a wide variety, but the company also has a distinct and separate military knife category where you can buy versions of the M9 Bayonet in OD green or black (available on Amazon.com for less than $100), the ASEK Air Force Rescue/Survival Blade, and the M7B M16 bayonet with the upgraded rubber handle. There are a number of other very cool fixed-blade knives in this category, such as the Tanto bayonet, which has a great penetrating point, and is otherwise configured like the M7B, and the OKC3S Marine bayonet.

The Marine bayonet brings me to a point about blade style. Part of the Marine blade is serrated, which means that you need a special sharpening tool (another damn thing to carry), to keep it operationally sharp. I would stick with a standard edge. They can be sharpened on a rock in an emergency, with much less time and effort involved.

Under Ontario's Spec Plus Next Generation line are several models that are updates of the original Ka-Bar fighting knives, as well as a tactical machete and its SPAX tomahawk-based rescue tool.

This last was designed for fire and rescue crews, but would also work for S.W.A.T. This brings me to another desirable form cutting tool that may be good to have along, the tactical tomahawk. The tomahawk is a very old combat tool (one very different from a hatchet), that disappeared from active combat basically at the end of our Indian wars. It was resurrected in a slightly modified form for use in combat and as a multi-tool during jungle warfare in Vietnam. Not long ago, tactical knifemaker SOG updated the Vietnam-era 'hawk in its Tactical Tomahawk and other variants, including a bright satin-finished version and the shorter handled, updated Voodoo Hawk. In the world of S.W.A.T., these 'hawks are often called "breaching 'hawks," since their primary function is to help break through light to moderate barriers during an emergency entry.

The 'hawks are one SOG product that is made in China, and they are priced under $70. I carried my full-size version on several S.W.A.T. missions. It is nice to see that SOG upgraded the holster from a basic ballistic nylon model to a hard nylon model, which should allow it to attach to MOLLE (Modular Lightweight Load-carrying Equipment, pronounced like the girl's name Molly), armor or a belt more efficiently. As I've said, anything you're going to pack along with you should have more than one purpose, and, obviously, the breaching 'hawk does, as it is also a devastating combat weapon for CQB. There are a number of tomahawk models and brands out there, but I think SOG fields one of the best and at a very reasonable price.

Machetes can be a candidate for inclusion in your survival bag, being very useful for hacking your way through brush or jungle. But, for a machete to be of real value in clearing it needs to be long, and that means it takes up a lot of room. If you feel you need one in your emergency evacuation gear, it should be attached to your pack. And, if you aren't planning on getting to your shelter-in-place site by hacking through undergrowth, you won't need one, and it will end up being extra weight that doesn't get used much.

If you want to split the difference between the supportive tools like the chisel-pointed MAK1 rescue knife and the machete or tactical tomahawk, take a look at the BLACKHAWK! Small Pry rescue tool. The Small Pry is short enough to carry MOLLE'd onto a tactical vest or armor, but thick enough to handle most prying chores. It also has a fixed cutting blade portion that can be used for chopping, as well as emergency defense. BLACKHAWK! Also has some excellent fixed-blade survival/tactical knives under the $200 price tag. All its products are winners and good investments.

One other area I want to touch on briefly falls into the small pocket variety, tools that are really, well, tools. While the pocket tool has no combat utility, they will prove vital to making life easier. Obviously you can't pack your tool box with you if you have to evacuate, so you do need something of quality manufacture to fulfill this role. Again, don't rely on a no-name brand of tool that is pre-packaged in a survival kit. Instead, select and pay for your own tool separately.

There are just two types of pocket tools I wish to mention, the genuine Swiss Army Knife (Wenger versions are less expensive than Victorinox), and the plier multi-tool as first made by Leatherman. In either category, go with the middle range of tools on each type. If you go full bore, then the tool no longer is a "pocket" tool, and if you get too few tools, you are really only equipped with either a pocket knife or set of pliers. For the Swiss Army Knife, I like the model that has scissors, awl, and Phillips and two sizes of flathead screwdrivers, in addition to the bottle and can opener. I favor the Gerber Multiplier for a multi-tool. It has some of the same tools that the Swiss Army knife does, plus needle-nose pliers and Fiskars-brand scissors.

Less-Lethal Options

So far we've been discussing only deadly force options in terms of firearms and the support tools that could be used to deliver lethality in CQB situations. But there may be times when using deadly force is not the most desirable way of dealing with the situations.

Two great survival knives. On the left is Smith & Wesson's Search and Rescue fixed-blade knife. High quality at a very reasonable price, the sheath also holds a sharpening stone. On the right is the Columbia River Knife and Tool MAK-1 Rescue Tool. Designed by Canadian firefighter James McGowan, the chisel-shaped end is designed for prying, while the pommel is designed for undoing battery cables on automobiles and for breaking out car windows with its carbide tip.

The MAK-1 Rescue Tool and Extrik-8-R seatbelt cutter, both available from CRKT in original bright stainless or subdued tactical black. New sheaths are kydex and can be mounted on body armor, backpacks, etc.

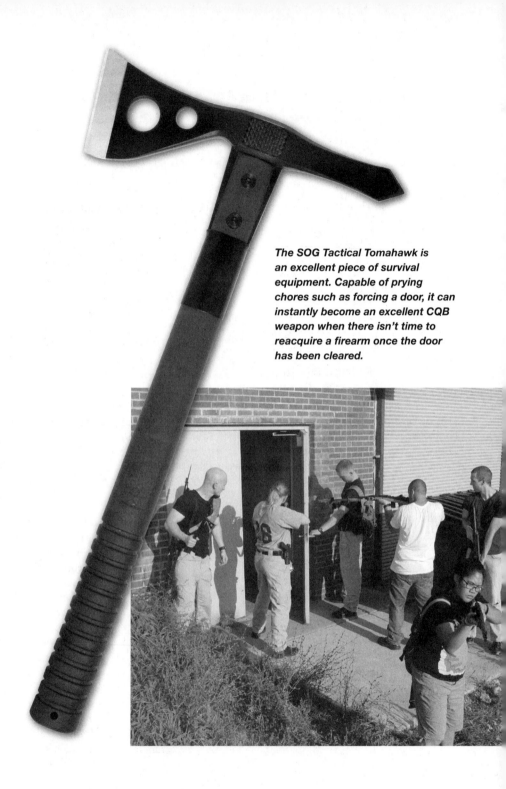

The SOG Tactical Tomahawk is an excellent piece of survival equipment. Capable of prying chores such as forcing a door, it can instantly become an excellent CQB weapon when there isn't time to reacquire a firearm once the door has been cleared.

"Less lethal" is the current in-vogue term used to describe an application of force that is not intended or designed to cause death. The terms used to be "non-lethal" or "less than lethal," but it came to be recognized that sometimes a force application as simple as a punch to an opponent's head can, and sometimes has, caused death. Thus, the term "less lethal" is very appropriate for a punch to the head, even if death was actually caused by the receiver of the punch falling and striking their head on a hard surface. By the way, less-lethal force applications can be seen as another way of layering your defense.

The first option available is in the form of crowd control OC (Oleoresin Capsicum) pepper spray. I'm not talking about the small key-ring units that go in a women's purse or on a police officer's belt, I'm referring to the types of sprays police use for crowd dispersal. For example, the website www.redhotpepperspray.com carries the Fox Labs Pistol Grip Crowd Control Canister, which looks like a small fire extinguisher and carries enough pressure to discharge multiple fog blasts of 5.3 million Scoville heat unit-rated OC pepper spray.

Fox Labs pepper sprays are miserable to be hit with. It causes swelling and closing of the eyes, coughing and choking, and intense burning of exposed skin. For deterring two- and four-legged aggressors that you may not want to kill, it is hard to beat. Note that this product can't be sold in jurisdictions where it currently is most needed, such as California, where for years civilians have been allowed to purchase only watered down pepper sprays or tear

Fox Labs' 5.3-million Scoville Heat Unit-rated crowd canister can propel its contents out to 20 feet. It is an excellent less-lethal weapon choice. Unfortunately, it's not legal everywhere, such as California. Make sure of your local laws before purchasing.

gas (after all you wouldn't want to injure someone who is attempting to rape you too badly). Make sure you are familiar with the laws in your local jurisdiction.

One other option that has emerged that has potential is the 37mm launcher system. These launchers have become popular of late for use with flares in international waters as defense against pirates. Firearms are illegal in international waters for everyone except pirates, so 37mm single-shot launchers firing burning signal flares can be quite a deterrent if they happen to land in some crappy, gasoline fume-filled pirate boat, or actually hit a pirate directly. Bates and Dittus makes some very reliable 37mm launchers in configurations that range from pistols to shoulder-fired launchers to the UBL37-a model that mimics the 40mm M203 grenade launcher and mounts under the barrel of a rail-equipped AR-type rifle.

The UBL is my favorite variant. Since it mounts to the bottom rail section of any AR-15 with a railed fore-end, the M4 military-contoured barrel is an unnecessary feature to have on your AR. The UBL will work on any M4 configuration barrels, pencil thin barrels, or heavy barrels. The type of barrel plays no part in the attaching.

Before we get into any further discussion of 37mm launchers, you need to be aware of federal law regarding these devices. First, they are totally legal for civilian ownership as long as you don't possess law enforcement-type impact or specialty rounds such as wooden baton rounds, rubber pellet rounds, or tear gas rounds. This is important. Possession by civilians of impact rounds or rounds designed to cause even less lethal injury to humans changes the previously legal launcher to an ATF Prohibited Destructive Device. These restrictions leave flare and smoke rounds as being legal for civilian ownership. For best results in a legal defense, spend the money and get military- or police-quality smoke rounds or flares. If you can't find true 37mm police-grade flares, obtain a supply of 26.5mm or 12-gauge signal flares and the adaptors for the 37mm chamber. Since there are more 37mm flares, smoke, and bird bomb cartridges available now, it may be wise to test a few of them, as well. Most rounds travel beyond 400 feet, giving the user a good standoff distance from which to illuminate the threat. If you can find parachute flares, you have the capability of longer-term threat illumination.

One of the best things about the UBL37 launcher is the operational system. It does not cock on closing or opening. There is a lever on the right side of the frame above the trigger that must be pulled back for cocking. There is also a separate safety lever on that side. This means that the UBL37 can be kept loaded but un-cocked for as long as you deem necessary without fear of an accidental discharge. The trigger is smooth and easy to pull.

Even without the availability of tear gas or impact rounds, firing flares, bird bombs, or smoke rounds at or around dangerous groups can certainly distract them and disrupt them away from their original intent. In fact, it may leave them wondering what rounds will be launched at them next, especially since the Bates and Dittus UBL looks just like the military M203.

For police operations, I have my launcher attached to a custom 5.56mm Sun Devil/CMMG carbine. It is kept loaded with a bean bag round and is sighted using a Lasermax Universal Green Laser on the upper rail length. That way I have the ability to deliver a bean bag or other round in lieu of deadly force, but the deadly force is right there if need be. The operational systems are so vastly different that I have no fears of accidentally activating the wrong weapon system under a stressful situation. Other S.W.A.T. cops I've shown the setup to have universally said "That's badass!"

The addition of the UBL37 makes the standard M4 absolutely

fearsome with that big extra barrel located under the little 5.56mm one and it may serve to provide an extra level of intimidation that could just preclude having to actually fire any round at all in defense. There is only one downside to attaching the launcher and that is that it adds four pounds of weight to your M4. For me this means no other accessories on the gun other than the Lasermax sight. (The open sights I use on this M4 are the Diamond Sights from Diamondhead Tactical. Quick to pick up and align, the Diamond Sights are a new generation of what I call "stand-alone backup iron sights." Yes they can fold out of the way, but they can be used without being secondary to optical sights.) With no other attachments other than a Tactical Link single-point sling, this setup is manageable.

The UBL37 has a 12-inch barrel and will handle up to eight-inch-long law enforcement-only shells, such as wooden baton rounds. Both the 37mm flare and smoke rounds are much shorter than law enforcement impact rounds and don't need a 12-inch barrel to shoot properly. With this in mind, plus the fact that the long rounds aren't civilian legal, Bates and Dittus has just introduced a nine-inch barrel UBL37 to save weight for civilian users. Weight savings is approximately one pound, which really makes the load much lighter. I haven't gotten to work with the shorter-barreled version, as it was just becoming available as I write this, but I can vouch for B&D quality, and if I wanted one of these launchers only for use with

Having a Bates and Dittus UBL37 mounted under an AR-15 acts as an intimidation force multiplier. Aggressors don't need to know that either less lethal or civilian legal flares or explosives will be launched, rather than the high explosive military rounds that the 40mm M203 grenade launcher shoots. The author's UBL is mounted to his custom CMMG mid-length 5.56mm Sun Devil custom lower via a rail-to-rail adaptor. Note the Lasermax green laser on the top rail of the UBL37; the author's AR is otherwise kept light, since the UBL37 weighs four pounds. Diamond iron sights are by Diamondhead Tactical.

Top Left: Loading the UBL 37 is similar to loading an M203 launcher. Its latch releases the barrel/chamber assembly, which then slides forward. A round is dropped in and the barrel slid back until it latches.

Top Right: To fire the UBL37, the cocking latch on the right side must be pulled back and the safety taken off. For law enforcement use, this feature is a plus, since a live less-lethal round can be carried chambered but un-cocked until needed. The military 40mm M203 cocks on loading.

Left: The author launches a civilian legal smoke round from the UBL37 downrange at a distance of 300 feet. Quality 37mm rounds are usually good for a 450-foot maximum range.

civilian rounds, I would definitely opt for the new nine-inch model.

There are other launchers on the market. Some of them are foreign imports and some are lighter, but considering the fact that you can beat someone senseless with a B&D and not hurt the launcher,

that's the way I'd go. B&D also markets a stock conversion kit for the UBL37 so you can fire it from the shoulder if you don't want to leave it on your M4. While I wouldn't equip every M4 I had with one, it does add a bit of additional "force multiplier" ability to your survival armory.

The white smoke 37mm rounds could be used to disrupt or discourage aggressive groups of people without having to result to lethal force. Remember that a smoke or flare round striking someone in the head could prove lethal and that flare rounds fired on the ground can start fires.

With a 12-gauge or, in this case, a 26.5mm adaptor, other civilian-legal rounds can be fired from the UBL or ExD launchers. Do not get a 12-gauge adaptor and fire standard 12-gauge slug or shot rounds. That is illegal, since you just turned a signaling device into a firearm (read that as a "zip gun"). Also, keep in mind that 37mm shells are all blackpowder charged, so standard factory 12-gauge smokeless rounds are of much higher pressure. Here a 26.5mm maritime signaling flare is loaded into a B&D Adaptor. After firing, empty shell casings drop free from the launcher when the barrel is opened (top right).

The new Bates & Dittus nine-inch UBL37 is shown mounted on the author's M4. The full-size UBL37 is shown with the M4 stock and pistol grip conversion kit attached. The 12-inch UBL37 can fire long 37mm rounds as shown standing in front of the author's pack to the left of the short 37mm rounds. The latter is the only size digestible in the nine-inch UBL37.

Chapter 9

AMMUNITION CONSIDERATIONS

By now you have probably noticed that I've left out of these discussions one type of ammunition and weapons system, and that is the rimfire.

When times are hard and dangerous, having a rimfire weapon, specifically a .22 LR rimfire weapon, will not only be handy, but possibly downright necessary. There are several reasons for this.

First, there may be times when you want to keep the noise level down and not draw a bunch of attention to your location. I can tell you that living out in the country, an unsuppressed .22 can be heard from quite a ways away, not as long away as a centerfire pistol, rifle, or shotgun, but it's still audible. This may mean that, if you can afford it and want to get the tax stamp for one, a suppressor might be a good idea to dampen the noise even further.

Second, you may want to have a lighter weapon to take small game with for supplementing your food supply. The .22 LR is the best choice for this, as it is truly a universal round and available in many different configurations, and anything larger will destroy too much meat, a crucial component of your survival that will be at a premium.

Third, children or members of your party who are recoil-sensitive may be better served with a .22 for their defense. They will certainly be able to carry a lot of ammo for a long distance in a very small space. Summed up, the .22 LR is a necessity.

As I see it, there are two ways to go with the .22. Over the last couple years, replica .22s, built as close as possible to mimic or serve as sub-caliber understudies to their full-size cousins, have become extremely popular. I have worked with some really great representatives of this type. Given the right brand and model, many are nearly indistinguishable from the centerfire versions, down to operating controls, size, and weight. A particularly popular weapon that has been made over into a .22 LR version is the AR-15. Smith & Wesson, Colt's, and several other AR makers have rimfire versions of their centerfire lines, usually made under license agreement with other companies who specialize in these types of weapons, and they are definitely true to the originals. There are also a plethora of .22 LR uppers or conversion kits that can be dropped onto an existing centerfire lower.

For playtime, such systems work fine. For survival time, I want a dedicated rifle and don't want to have to switch things off and on. To that end, one of the rimfire ARs that I *don't* like is the model made by Ruger. Instead of developing a new rifle or contracting the job out to another manufacturer, Ruger opted to build its model around its own fine 10/22 rifle, keeping the controls of that rifle intact. While I'm sure this works in terms of being a fun shooter, it certainly doesn't serve as a trainer or potential fighting weapon, because it doesn't operate like a real AR. Much the same can be said of the Mossberg Tactical .22. Neither it nor the Ruger are the close copy of the AR that the Colt's and Smith & Wesson models are. The Colt's version, made by the German firm Umarex, is the most accurate copy of them all, with several variants, including a full-size rifle, available. Umarex also make a great copy of the Colt 1911 pistol.

One of the best producers of .22 LR replica guns is German Sport Guns (GSG). Its GSG 522 is an outstanding semi-auto copy of the MP5. I had one that I unfortunately had to sell at a cash-strapped point in time. Equipped with a 25-round magazine, it was the most reliable semi-automatic .22 rifle I think I have ever handled. I took it to a .22-only match at a nearby range. It never missed a beat, while other folks fielding customized Ruger 10/22s with extended magazines experienced regular jams. Controls and charging operation on the GSG 522 were exactly the same as on an MP5. GSG also makes an excellent 1911, the GSG-5. With a frame made of Zamak alloy, it imparts the solid feel of the 1911 without the expense. Equipped with adjustable combat sights, beavertail grip safety, curved mainspring housing, and combat trigger, the GSG-5 is an excellent sidearm in and of itself.

Of big news from GSG is its upcoming Stg44 .22 replica. A copy of the German assault rifle that appeared too late at the end of WWII to help the German Army (good thing), it did spawn the development of the AK-47 by Mikhail Kalishnikov two years after the war ended. I am awaiting a copy of that rifle for testing, but if it's anything like the other GSG products, I'm sure it will not disappoint. Speaking of AKs, GSG also has a .22 variant of that weapon.

Chiappa is another big player in the .22 replica market. I have one of its replica M1 Carbines. A dead ringer for later production M1s, it features a faux plastic bayonet lug (I tried to fit a real

The .22 LR round and its firearms aren't just for recreational fun. Ammunition is inexpensive to practice with and, as we all know, practice makes perfect. Both pistols and rifles chambered in .22 LR make super platforms for practicing marksmanship drills and honing the basics like trigger and sight control, but they can also be the weapon of choice for small-statured adults and youths in your group, especially those adverse to heavy recoil and noise.

bayonet on it and it didn't work), adjustable rear sight, a rotating lever safety that replaced the original push-button type, and a plastic 10-round magazine that mimics the appearance of a real carbine mag, with the exception that there's no slit to reveal the round count. The first edition I tested had some functionality issues. Chiappa sent out a second one, and although I haven't had time to work with it much, it doesn't seem to have the same issues as the first pre-production carbine did. I am sure that, with Chiappa's fine reputation, you can count on the reliability of its weapons, and for survival, reliability is everything.

The replica .22 concept has a lot going for it in terms of survival weapon use, both as a sub-caliber trainer and, of course, as a weapon for the recoil-shy. The .22 will acquit itself well against human targets out to 150 yards, at the very least getting the attention of anyone struck with it, and there are a lot of great modern loads out there for this round. I would favor any high-velocity loading that has a solid bullet. As you may have to shoot at targets behind cover or who may be wearing heavy clothing, it is imperative to get as much penetration from the .22 as possible, particularly if penetration of bone is called for. If it will function in your gun, the Remington Viper truncated-cone solid-point is one of my favorites. In any event, you want to make sure your .22 will function with anything and everything you can run through it, as you may be scrounging for ammo if the calamity is extended, which brings me to the other type of rimfire, the traditional .22.

When I say "traditional" .22, I mean the basic semi-autos like the Ruger 10/22 with its 10-shot rotary magazine (though, from what I've observed, the 10/22 may not like aftermarket extended magazines), Marlin's line of semi-autos, which I have found to be reliable, and other common manually operated repeaters.

I favor the lever-action rifles. The lever-action Marlin 39, for instance, was the first gun I ever shot. Over the years it proved to be a very accurate and highly reliable firearm. I don't remember an occasion where it ever jammed. One of the Marlin's best features is the tubular magazine. With the tube design, there's usually a capacity of somewhere around 15 rounds of .22 LR, but there is an even higher capacity for .22 Short or Long rounds, usually around 20. If you want a quieter round, primer-driven CB rounds are available, as well. These make excellent pest-control or ultra-quiet target rounds. These lesser rounds won't function in an autoloader or any gun with a fixed magazine, but will in the few tube-fed bolt-action guns you might find out there. Beyond this, I think the very best advantage that a tubular magazine offers over a box design is that you can't lose it or leave it behind. It stays with the gun.

Henry Repeating Arms makes some of the best modern .22 lever-action rifles out there at a reasonable price. More compact and less expensive than the Marlin 39, the blued steel, round-barrel H001 Henry Carbines is my top choice for a survival .22. Light and easily handled in tight spaces, the H001 holds 15 rounds of. 22 LR and 21 rounds of .22 Short. The manual operation eliminates the reliability issues encountered with any semi-auto shooting standard velocity ammunition. Henry also markets the old AR-7 .22 Air Force survival rifle that can be stowed in its own buttstock for travel, but I find it a very clunky gun to handle. If you find one, try it out for yourself. You may be less finicky and it may fit in your survival plans better, but for me I will stay old school and go with the tube-fed lever-action .22

Centerfire Ammo— This is Self-Defense, Not Hunting

To emphasize, you are not choosing calibers for varmint, deer, or duck hunting, when we're talking about centerfire ammunition. You are choosing calibers for weapons that will help you and your family survive in dire circumstances. The calibers you select must be in common use by police and military personnel, as well in common sporting use for civilians. There are tons of great calibers and weapons out there, but only a handful will or should make it to your survival must-have list.

But picking the right caliber for your survival weapon is not enough. You also need to pick the right bullet type. For many of the highly touted brands out there, a lot of thought and calcula-

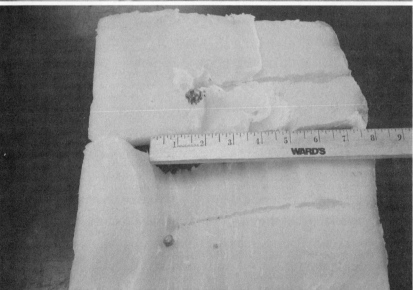

FN's Five-seveN holds a whopping 21 rounds of 5.7x28mm in a lightweight, reliable, blowback design. Penetration in gelatin is comparable to a 127-grain 9mm +P Ranger load. The question to ask is, can you find a constant and reliable source of the 5.7 round?

tion has gone into the projectiles that sit atop the case awaiting your launch command. Make no mistake, these are excellent loads and will likely perform well or very well, but they are all expensive. Few of us can afford to stockpile rounds like the 5.56mm TAP round by Hornady (heck, not many police departments that use TAP as a duty round can either). Check any police armory and you'll find that, by far, most rifle or pistol loads will be of the FMJ (full metal jacket) or ball variety. Unless you have all kinds of extra funds available, this is the ammo type you would want to stockpile for long-term survival—and there's not a thing wrong with that choice.

Every army in every major war from the start of the twentieth century until now has used ball ammo in their battle rifles and service pistols, with little complaint concerning lack of effectiveness. (The few exceptions may be the .30 Carbine, but only when used against the North Koreans and Chinese at extended range when they were wearing their winter coats. Even that's in dispute, as most of our troops were, by then, using the full-auto M2 carbine—some have surmised that many of the rounds thought to have struck home actually missed, thus skewing the impression of effectiveness). In any event there was no question of stopping power with ball ammo of the .45 ACP, .30-06, 7.62mm NATO (.308), and the 5.56mm NATO when it was first introduced. It has only been since Mogadishu and the Blackhawk incident that the stopping power of the 5.56 has been called into question. There are several reasons for that impression I think are worth examining.

During the early years of the Vietnam War, the barrel twist rate of the original 20-inch M16 barrel was 1:14 inches, which caused the 55-grain 5.56mm round to be on the edge of instability in flight. When it struck a soft target (read that as "people"),

A 1:14 twist AR-15/M16 barrel can effectively and accurately handle only 55-grain or lighter bullets. Heavier bullet weights, such as 62-grainers, become unstable in flight, tumbling as they traverse their path and striking targets, such as this car door, sideways. Wounds from tumbling rounds can be devastating, but accuracy is somewhat compromised. Remember, gotta make it to the target to get the job done.

it would tumble, thus causing the bullet to travel through flesh either sideways, blunt base first, or some combination thereof, thus causing a more severe wound. Not content with "if it works don't fix it," the Army claimed that cold arctic weather caused the bullet to become unstable in flight and then mandated a change to a 1:11 twist rate for the M16A1, which reduced the instability in arctic air and improved accuracy, but apparently didn't totally do away with all the tumbling propensity, although most wounds were not nearly as devastating.

After Vietnam, the Marines wanted more accuracy and better long-range penetration from the 5.56mm on Soviet personnel armor at extended ranges. In order to accomplish this, the Marines specified a 20-inch heavy barrel, a 1:7 twist, and a 62-grain steel core bullet for the M16A2. They got more accuracy, and a weapon that was nearly three pounds heavier than the original M16, but any tumbling potential was gone. The 5.56 M16A2 punched a 5.56mm hole going in and the same size hole going out; it was a much less devastating weapon. In Mogadishu, our troops, armed with M16A2s, faced the slightly built Somali population, whose people tend to have a very low muscle mass. This gave the 5.56mm less opportunity to inflict severe wounds compared to the same round impacting a heavily muscled person. Also, many Somalis were high on the local drug "khat," which reduced their sensitivity to pain. These factors combined to reduce the ability of our troops to instantly incapacitate their attackers.

Fast forward to Afghanistan. Our troops have been faced with opponents with physical features similar to the Somalis and who have large amounts of locally grown opium available to them. The 20-inch barrel of the M16A1 and A2 was reduced to 16 inches on the now generally issued M4 Carbine, thus dropping velocity a couple hundred feet per second, perhaps more, over the A1 and A2 rifles. On top of that, engagement distances over desert and mountain terrain were much greater than encountered in previous battles involving the M16. The 5.56mm round simply ran out of gas. Going from the 62-grain ball round to a 77-grain Black Hills boat-tail hollowpoint has, according to my Special Forces source, served to resolve those issues without the need of switching to the 6.8 SPC or other round.

The 55-grain 5.56mm round, particularly when fired out of a 20-inch barrel, should prove quite effective when fired within its

300-meter effective range. I have searched for, but haven't found, someone making a 1:14 twist AR barrel and upper, and I would love to try one with 5.56mm ammo. That combination should prove to eliminate the need for expensive expanding ammo. Even though I can't get one, I am still satisfied with ball 5.56mm performance out of my 20-inch rifle and, for that matter, my M4 in general. For duty use I am required to use controlled-expansion rounds like the Hornady TAP, which isn't an issue, since my agency provides the ammo and under our current conditions law enforcement must be concerned about the potential for unintended collateral damage. Following collapse, though, that issue tends to disappear, both for civilians and cops who may find that their agency has run out of their limited supplies of controlled-expansion ammo and ball ammo is all that they have left. It also won't matter for officers who have abandoned their posts to protect their families.

When it comes to larger-diameter rounds like the .30 Carbine, 7.62x39mm, and bigger, there are few folks who bother purchasing controlled-expansion rounds unless they use these cartridges for hunting. Often, ball rounds can be purchased on sale in bulk amounts of 500 or so at a very low per-round cost. A bargain it may be, but it's here I'll throw out three cautionary issues.

Bulk purchase cartridges in calibers used by former Soviet Bloc countries are often corrosive in nature. In the past, some of these rounds have been labeled as "low corrosive" or with some other such misleading term to boost their sale. There is no such thing—corrosive is corrosive. The corrosive component of such rounds is the primer, specifically primers using the old fulminate of mercury to prompt the power ignition, rather than more modern materials like lead styphnate and others. The only way to re-

ally clean the weapon and stop corrosion once these rounds have been fired is to strip the weapon and flush with hot soapy water like you would a blackpowder weapon, or to use a cleaning agent designed to remove the mercury fouling.

When these rounds were used in bolt-action weapons, cleaning was relatively simple and only the barrel itself needed attention. In guns like the AK-47 or SKS, though, not only the barrel needs to be cleaned, but also the gas piston system and housing. No thanks, count me out. Remember, the former Soviet Army didn't care what they shot out their guns. Those firearms were so cheap to manufacturer that, if corrosion became a problem, they

These are mostly mid-range rifle cartridges. Starting from the left: 124-grain FMJ 9mm; 165-grain FMJ .40 S&W (stay away from the 180-grain bullet for carbines, they don't have sufficient velocity to shoot flat and extend the range of the round, which is why the .45 ACP is not in the lineup); 5.7x28mm JHP; Winchester 110-grain JHP +P+ "Treasury Load" .38 Special; 110-grain FMJ .30 U.S. Carbine; 158-grain JSP .357 Magnum; 55-grain FMJ 5.56mm; 123-grain FMJ 7.62x39mm loaded in a steel case. The last two are traditional, full-power battle cartridges. The first is the 147-grain FMJ 7.62 NATO (aka .308 Winchester), and the second is the granddaddy of them all, the 150-grain FMJ .30-06 M1 Garand load.

would make a new one or replace the corroded parts. Or maybe they didn't even concern themselves. You don't have that luxury. Pay a few more bucks and get non-corrosive ammo from a trusted source.

My second concern about bulk ball ammo concerns the powders they use. Cheap, Russian-manufactured 5.56mm ammo I've fired uses cheap powder that shoots dirty. The last thing a direct-gas AR-15 needs is more powder fouling blown into the action. Before you buy any of it in bulk, try some out in small quantities. The increased fouling doesn't bother an AK or SKS, but I promise you it will eventually make most ARs unhappy.

There is some disagreement on this next point, depending on what manufacturer or armorer you ask, but I tend to play it safe, and so I'll tell you not to use steel-cased ammo in an AR. It is, without a doubt, harder on the extraction system, which was designed to work with brass. I don't believe this to be an issue on the robust AK-47, which may have taken the use of steel-cased ammo into consideration in its design, as brass was in short supply near the end of WWII.

There are other issues with steel ammo beyond the extractor. Some of the cases that are polymer coated to be easier on extractors can have that polymer begin to soften in rapid fire as the gun heats up. Some brands used zinc-washed cases to protect from steel to steel contact without the possibility of gumming things up; Hornady uses zinc on steel on its low-price practice ammo line. We used this ammo and Russian-made Silver Bear (not to be confused with Silver State Armory) zinc-plated ammo at my former sheriff's office qualification back when brass ammo was in short supply during the start of the Iraq war. The ammo is fine until it's opened and left exposed to the air for awhile, but even when kept in our climate-controlled armory, these rounds developed a powdery white oxidation on the cases. I refused to run the stuff through my personal rifle during qualification. Maybe it wasn't an issue, but I didn't want to risk it.

In summary, purchase only non-corrosive ball ammo, brass cased, and of a known brand or source for your defensive stores. If you have some of the really el-cheapo stuff on hand or you just want to plink, use it (not the corrosive stuff though) and then tend to the cleaning of your guns. For pistols, I also avoid steel-cased stuff, but Speer's aluminum-cased Blazer ammo is satisfactory. Aluminum is actually softer than brass and won't harm extractors, although the aluminum case dents a little more easily than brass if you drop it on a hard surface. Blazer has been time tested and used by police agencies to save funds during qualifications for at least 20 years. If you can find it, get it. The same cautions goes for shotguns. There are some cheap brands of foreign manufactured shotshells that use steel for the cartridge case heads instead of brass. Do what you want, but I won't use that in my defensive shotguns, especially ones that don't have Mil-Spec parts.

About Stopping Power

Some of you reading this will have concerns about the stopping capability of FMJ rounds, and those concerns are valid. No FMJ round will be as destructive in tissue as an expanding bullet, with the exception of FMJ rounds out of the 1:14 twist M16 or the police-only armor-piercing 5.7x28mm rounds which also tumbles in soft tissue. I tested some of those AP rounds out of the FNH-USA Five-seveN pistol into a cylinder of ballistic media. One penetrated six inches, tumbled, and blew out the top of the tube of media (perhaps sideways) and bounced off the ceiling of the indoor police range. The hole it blew in the media was three inches-plus in diameter—that should tend to take care of most threats.

Quality controlled-expansion rounds such as the Hornady TAP

line do a great job. The Columbus, Ohio, Police S.W.A.T. team has found that a three-round burst of TAP in a charging pit bull does a better job of stopping them "dead in their tracks" than 00 Buckshot and it doesn't over-penetrate like buckshot will. Like I said, if you can afford those rounds over FMJ 5.56mm buy them, but if you can't, then ball is your round of choice. And do this. Practice all you can on silhouette targets aiming for the heart/spine and head areas. It may take more rounds to do the job than the expanding rounds, but it will do the job. It is going to end up being an issue of quantity going down range, not the individual quality of each bullet. Suppressive fire isn't cheap, and barrier penetration is going to be a more important component of those rounds than expansion in soft targets. It will be a different world.

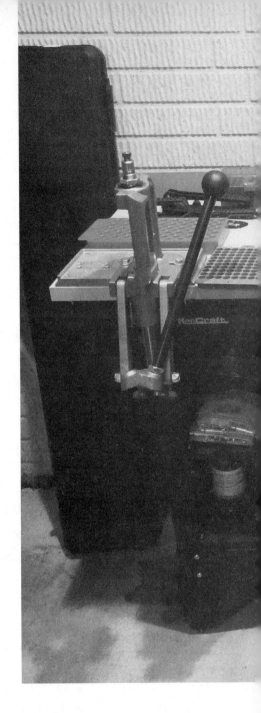

Building a supply of ammo is imperative. A well-equipped loading bench like this will be a boon to those who can afford it and have the know-how to load safe, good quality ammo. If you buy ammo from a loading buddy, make sure it's good quality stuff, both safe and reliable through your guns.

Chapter 10

OFF-DUTY CARRY FOR THE 21ST-CENTURY COP

In case you didn't know it, there are boatloads of cops out there who now believe in what we are talking about, the concept that society is on the edge of imminent collapse unless things take an immediate turn-around. Not one of us wants to see this happen. We have sworn an oath to protect and defend the Constitutions of our individual states and the United States. We—at least the cops from my generation—love and respect our nation and its traditions, things we want to see continued and strengthened, but we are preparing for the worst, and hoping for the best. This includes cops who never gave much thought to politics in the past, cops who have surprised me when they expressed their concerns and said that they, too, were preparing. I say this to inform the reader that this is not just a concern of the civilian world or the Tea Party or whatever. This concern reaches across all strata.

An example of teamwork by a S.W.A.T. team clearing a stairwell. Note that all angles and personnel are covered through the use of multiple firearms types, in the case a rifle and shotgun pointing up and, though you can't see it, a handgun aimed down at the landing.

All this brings me to the point of off-duty carry for the readers of this book who are law enforcement. I have been a cop for 32 years and a police firearms instructor for 26 of those. For all of those 32 years, I have carried a handgun off-duty nearly every day, but have seen other cops in my own agencies go carelessly about their days not carrying at all. As a police academy commander for 21 years of my career, I have preached to those students the *imperative* requirement that they carry off-duty at all times. Ever since 9/11, that has included in church, which I didn't do previously. Take into account the skyrocketing number of psychotic shooter attacks, with a concomitant increase the last few years of shooting attacks on police officers, and my off-duty carry, as well as that of numerous other cops, begins with an off-duty AR-15 stowed in the trunk of my vehicle. It is what I recommend to my cadet classes, as well. I still carry a pistol on my person, of course, but that's going to be used in an emergency, when I am too far away to access to my rifle.

The rifle I have at the ready in my vehicle is just that, a rifle. And I have one in each vehicle. The first is a full-size AR-15 A2 configuration by Del-Ton, while the other is my aforementioned favorite, the Century International Arms CA-15. I have qualified with both guns. There are plenty of spare magazines stashed in the excellent Drago rifle case. The rifles are stock; no lights or optics. Their carry slings are standard military. The only aftermarket add-on I've opted for is the XS Sight Systems tritium stripe front sight on the Del-Ton rifle. Either of these iron-sighted rifles allows me to fire accurately at long range, and while I might not be able to *easily* make a 300-meter headshot with this setup, I can certainly hit the rest of the body. Nothing to turn on or off, flip up, or close. Just take the rifle out, pull the charging handle, and fire.

While I prefer the full-length rifle, since the longer sight radius helps me to maintain a sharp sight picture, an M4-style carbine works well, too. For example, DPMS makes the AP4 A3-style carbine. A3 weapons have the removable carry handle that allows alternate access to the Picatinny rail hidden underneath. The AP4 is essentially the same as the military M4 with two exceptions. First, of course, it is semi-auto only. Second, the round, military-style front handguards are the DPMS patented Glacier Guards, designed to dissipate heat through long rapid-fire sessions.

The advantage that the M4/AP4 has, of course, is that it will take up less space in your trunk or vehicle interior. Make sure you have passe your agency's annual qualification with your rifle, as you are carrying it as a perilous times off-duty weapon.

Should your agency not authorize rifles, there is always the shotgun. Get the model your department carries and set it up in the same configuration as the issue-duty version. Having a good supply of rifled slugs with it is imperative, as this is the weapon that you may have to go up against an active shooter with, and buckshot probably won't get it done when the range gets long. It should have rifle sights on it, rather than just a bead for precision. A bandolier full of spare ammo to throw over your shoulder is important, as well. BLACK-HAWK! Makes a bandolier that holds 90 rounds, enough to keep most bad guys plenty busy.

While a five-shot .38 on the body, with reloads, still makes an excellent off-duty piece, it is really not enough, especially if you don't carry a rifle in your vehicle. You may need to carry a larger handgun with more ammo, and I understand that certain weather conditions, like the heat of summer may not make this practical or comfortable. For times like that and while on vacation, I will still use a fanny pack due to its convenience, and especially for use in areas where there are a lot of tourists, because I'll stick out less. For other times and locations, the shoulder sling packs, like Maxpedition's Sitka, are a better answer.

The Sitka is an absolutely *outstanding* sling pack for short-term use. In my case, the Sitka, which is larger than the Versa-Pack series, is set up for left shoulder carry since I am right-handed. Once slung that way, just snap together the cross-chest strap and off you go. If you need to carry it longer term, you can also sling it over your head for a kind of cross-body carry. Inside the pack there's a compartment for your handgun—you will need to get Maxpedition's Universal Velcro Holster to complete the package—as well as compartments

Shotguns like the Ithaca 37 Defense pump-action can also be carried off duty. Extra ammo will be needed, such as the rifled slugs that can be seen here in the stock carrier. Note: Unless you are proficient with only a front bead, rifle sights are preferred.

The Maxpedition Sitka features a special pouch for securing handguns. Other compartments are for storage, and there's even one for a hydration bladder. There are plenty of MOLLE body armor attachment points available, and the forest green color blends in everywhere.

for spare ammo, another large pocket for adding a hydration bladder (there's an area at the top to pull the tube through), MOLLE attachment points on the strap and body of the pack, and clever ways of blocking access to certain compartments by pickpockets. There's also an outer Velcro area for attaching a name tag or other identification. The back of the pack is padded for comfort against your body.

The Sitka isn't just for weapons carry. There is a side pocket for a water bottle or maybe a radio, and it's great for carrying other emergency supplies (protein bars, small first aid kit, etc.), in case the balloon goes up away from home. It's not too bulky or attention getting. I carried mine into a trendy deli here in town the other day without a look. Inside was a Beretta M9A1, among the other supplies. While

The BLACKHAWK! sling pack is easy to carry and contains one large main compartment, with a smaller compartment on the front and a smaller section inside. This pack is strictly for gear; there is no specialized holster compartment. It rides very well.

Maxpedition makes larger packs, for this use I wouldn't go larger. Larger packs, such as the BLACKHAWK! Sling Pack and some even bigger, can be kept in your vehicle stored with other emergency survival gear. Maxpedition and BLACKHAWK! gear is top of the line. Stay away from the cheap copies. Also, stay away from the Army Digital-style packs unless you're in the army or on a S.W.A.T. team that uses that camouflage pattern, as it attracts attention.

In addition to the firearm, off-duty carry has always mandated that other equipment be available to deal with off-duty occurrences, and these items can play into your emergency survival plans. First on the list are less-lethal options, such as a baton or the same chemical spray your department issues. A good flashlight is also a must. I love tactical flashlights, especially high-end, quality, American-made ones such as those produced by Streamlight, Sure-Fire, and First Light USA. I always have some sort of small tactical flashlight in the 120- to 200-lumen range in my pocket. However, while these lights will support you very well for a while when calamity strikes, they were born of and bred for a different mission. They heat up very fast if left on long-term due to their very high intensity levels (up to 600 to 900 lumens), and their reliance on CR123 lithium batteries gets expensive.

These lights are essential for police combat or tactical use, but they're not necessarily what you need for long-term illumination purposes. CR123 batteries, unless purchased online in bulk or at police supply stores are brutally expensive. Further, you can't find them everywhere. What you do need to keep in your vehicle or emergency packs are a few quality lights that use more conventional batteries—rechargeables are out of the question. If your car runs out of gas and you have to move on foot, the rechargeable is only going to last for an hour or so. Then all you're left with is an emergency impact device (read that as a club). Go with a modern, conventional battery-powered light instead of the CR123 or rechargeable styles.

One of the best examples of the breed (and which can well double as an emergency impact device) is the new Maglite 3D cell LED light. Featuring Maglite's famous, made-in-the-USA machined aircraft aluminium construction, this tried and true performer has been upgraded from its previously standard incandescent halogen bulb (with a spare in the tail-cap), to the modern, never-needs-replacing LED. Rated at a very bright 120-plus lumens, with a run time in the 70-hour range (though, of course, not at full power for the entire time), the Maglite eliminates the need for a charger, as well as expensive replacement batteries. You'll need one of these in either two or three cells kept in your vehicle or pack, with a few extra batteries on hand. You will have to check these batteries every once in awhile, since old school batteries will eventually leak acid if left untouched too long and ruin whatever electronics it touches. In addition to the light, don't forget a cutting tool of some sort. If you can fit it in your pack, a BLACKHAWK! Small Pry or MAK-1 rescue knife would come in handy.

If you're keeping extra weapons available to you in what I call "off-the-body" carry, where the gun is not physically at all times on your person, you need to be extra security conscious. There was a female chief of police in our area a few years ago who carried her gun in her purse when off-duty. One night she forgot her purse, leaving it in a public place. She realized her mistake after leaving and returned and got her purse—luckily with the gun still in it. To her credit, she gave herself three days off without pay as punishment. The situation could have been much worse had someone gotten her gun. If you are carrying a gun in a sling pack, it either needs to stay in your immediate reach or locked somewhere securely. You cannot afford to be forgetful with your hardware.

In your vehicle, your weapons need to be secured and out of sight. Some other things to consider about traveling with guns include:

1. Unless you keep your vehicle very close at hand, you should have the long gun securely locked in the trunk, with an additional locking mechanism that can actually be bolted to the body of the car or truck, such as those available from Santa Cruz Gunlocks.

2. Don't display any firearms or police-related decals on your car. It's like sticking a "Help yourself to my guns" sign on it.

3. How quickly can the weapon you selected safely be brought into action from a loaded or unloaded condition? Practice!

4. If the gun is kept in your vehicle long term, what are its maintenance requirements?

5. Don't use an expensive or irreplaceable long gun as your long-term off-duty rifle. It shouldn't break your bank or heart if stolen.

6. If you're a police officer with duty access to a full-auto weapon, don't make this your off-duty pick. Imagine, at the very least, the PR issues there, not to mention the time-off issues if it were to be stolen.

The need for every cop in the U.S. to carry the heaviest weapons possible while off-duty has never been more critical. It is a responsibility to yourself, the public and, most importantly, to your family. It is your responsibility to survive.

I will give those of you in law enforcement one last thing to think about. In the end, whose side will you be on? Will you, when calamity strikes, side with a government that orders the confiscation of law-abiding civilian weapons, such as happened during Katrina? And that's if you are still at your post and not protecting your own. Which side will win, the Constitution or the collapse?

Traveling—What's in *Your* Car Trunk?

Earlier on, I alluded to the concept of compact guns for travel and named a few that would work well: the Auto Ordnance M1A1 Folding Paratrooper; the Century International Arms UC9 Carbine; the Polish-made AKMS under-folder in 7.62x39mm; the Kel-Tec SUB-2000 9mm (I think the Kel-Tec in .40, in the long run, will be too high pressure for the design, just my guess, plus the 9mm shoots flatter); shotguns like the Mossberg 590A1 with the M4 carbine stock; the Marlin 1894C .357 lever-action carbine; and the various versions of M4-style carbines. All these arms are, of course, backed up by handguns.

This is a specific area of weapon, a type as exemplified by that list that, while compact in size, can deliver protective, suppressive fire-

Two semi-autos ready for travel, and both are bayonet capable. At bottom is the IO, Inc., Sporter, above it the Del-Ton 20-inch A2 AR-15. The Del-Ton rides with the author daily as a primary rifle. Either weapon would serve, but, for vacation travel, something more compact that attracts a little less attention would be preferable.

power from 100 to 200 meters and maybe more, depending on model and caliber. They are designed to be carried in a vehicle or RV with you while on vacation, encased in such a way as to not draw undue attention. The talk about undue attention is to avoid alarming folks, even those in gun-friendly areas. As a cop, I take seriously this level of care, since my home jurisdiction is many miles away and I won't be running across any officers that I personally know. *Especially* as a civilian, make sure you're aware of any and all state and local laws regarding the transportation of weapons through the places you travel. Some states don't recognize the Firearms Owners Protection Act of 1986, nor the lawsuits rendered against various jurisdictions for arresting and charging law-abiding citizens who drove through their boundaries legally armed. Because of the restrictions in New York and New Jersey, even as a cop I won't go there, first in protest, and second because I don't trust that all cops in those states will recognize my badge under the National Peace Officer Safety Act. Beyond that, there is just no reason to alarm the innocent, and you don't want people calling in on you as a potential active shooter.

Del-Ton builds excellent, relatively painlessly priced ARs. This one represents a good, multi-role setup.

The reason for the travel long gun is simply that we don't have any idea when the balloon will go up. I looked up the origin of that term, and it's a phrase that relates to the use of observation balloons in the first World War. The sight of such a balloon rising was nearly always followed by a barrage of shells soon after. The expression was reinforced during WWII, when the hoisting of barrage balloons was part of the preparations for an air raid. Further research indicated the term may even have gone back as far as the American Civil War, when observation balloons were first used. What the term and its origins all come down to, though, is that we can't be assured we'll remain secure in our safe houses and bunkers when a calamitous event occurs, and I sure as heck am not going to hang around in mine every day waiting for some future event, even if I was retired and could. Add in the additional variables such as whether the disaster will be more or less localized in nature (fire, flood, tornado, hurricane, unknown localized disorder), or one that is national (economic collapse), and you'll realize daily preparedness is crucial.

My carrying a long gun with me everywhere actually began while I was on the S.W.A.T. team at the Sheriff's office as both an entry officer and sniper. Since the likelihood existed and occurred on several occasions that I would have to respond from my full-time job if called out and would not have time to gear up, I just kept my gear with me. When I took my current position at the Village of Baltimore, Ohio, as a Sergeant, I kept carrying the long guns for the same reason. As a member of a small, village PD, I am available for call-out 24/7. I wanted then and want to now have an adequate tool for dealing with an active shooter or barricade-type event.

In addition to the original reasons for having it with me, having a long gun with me allows me a better chance of fighting my way out of a chaotic urban situation and making it back home, each day, every day. Too, I drive an hour each way to work every day, and I like vacationing in the contiguous states of Michigan, Indiana, and West Virginia, and often further away in Tennessee and North Carolina. On that note, I think there is more of a need for a long gun when going on an extended trip, such as on a vacation, when you are hours instead of minutes away from home. (Keep in mind, though, that this practice is valid only if we're talking about driving someplace, rather than flying.)

Getting back home from work in the event of sudden disaster requires more forethought and preparedness than just packing an off-duty or concealed carry handgun. The locale and habits of the population you travel through to get home will dictate just how much gear you will need in your vehicle with you daily. As you consider the choice of a long gun to pack with you for daily carry or extended travel, try not to select one that's expensive or irreplaceable. It shouldn't break your bank or heart if stolen. As with most of the other firearms I've recommended, keep these rifles or shotguns clear of add-ons so that they can be brought into action without turning anything on, adjusting anything, and diverting your focus to something other than your threat. Also, keep them light and easy to carry in case you end up on foot, and make sure they have a sling so you can actually carry them with some comfort. One of the reasons I like the A1 and A2 AR/M16s is that they have a carry handle, providing a second option for hauling over a long distance. M4 or A3 rifles without a handle are a pain to slog around over the miles.

While the Bushmaster Carbon 15 (above) and the .450 Bushmaster (below) make superb entry and S.W.A.T. team-utilized firearms, they are over-equipped for use as survival guns. You say you're still tempted? Then note that neither has a carry handle, not a smart move if you're traveling on foot over hill and dale.

Chapter 11

TACTICS

Now that you've obtained at least a part of your gear, we need to talk a bit more about tactics and how to deal with what may be coming.

Our weapon deployment, outside the use of a concealed handgun for defense against singular criminal attack, is going to occur when the 9-1-1 system and any sort of reasonable organized law enforcement response has been compromised. In the rural tornado belt of the Midwestern portion of the United States, tornados that bring destruction to human beings, their homes, businesses, and livelihoods are an almost routine matter. Particularly in light of the doubling of the U.S. population since the 1960s, there is more chance that a tornado is going to damage and affect some portion of the populace in that central U.S. region. In those regions, at least to date, there has been little evidence of unlawful activities, such as looting, in the aftermath of such a disaster; people have been too busy taking care of themselves and each other. Have you noticed that in those states, in areas where towns have been totally flattened, no one is out crying for help from FEMA? People there tend to pull together.

In these areas, during these events, the likelihood of even having to display a long gun is remote. But if such a need arose, if your guns have been plucked out of a closet and flung to another end of your county, you're in trouble. So I'd recommend that you buy the biggest, baddest fireproof safe you can afford. Based on testing, even if your safe is picked up and taken to Oz, it's unlikely its door will have been blown off. If I lived in that region, I'd make sure my safe was bolted to the basement floor as an additional precaution. (This also points out why you should have a long gun with you in your car when disaster strikes. In fact, if your safe *isn't* in the basement, it might prove to be a good idea to take one or two guns, kept at the ready, to the basement or cellar with you when taking cover from a storm.

I've just been talking about natural disasters in the Midwest. Disasters hit other places, of course, and, in some of them, the reaction by the populace is vastly different from the relative calm and common sense Midwest people seem to exhibit. Look at New Orleans and Hurricane Katrina. It was not only proof of how inept FEMA is when it comes to dealing with disaster, but it also showed what can happen when the local populace considers this sort of disaster as an invitation to help itself to other peoples stuff. It also demonstrated that local police *will* leave their post, and that still others will seize the only means of defense (the gun) from the defenseless (like 67-year-old women living alone and armed with a .38 revolver).

In Katrina or L.A. riot-type situations, it is much more likely you will need to at least brandish that firearm. "Brandishing' is a term used in some state or local laws that means, in reference to weapons, "to wave or flourish menacingly," and in those locales, it also generally means that doing so is illegal in many circumstances. In some places, such as Washington, D.C, brandishing is likely illegal no matter what

In situations such as civil unrest and natural disaster, where rioting occurs, power grids are down, and fires are widespread, emergency help from law enforcement is hours or days away from responding, if at all. You must have your team organized before such events happen, practice for each scenario you can think of, and know whether you should stay and defend or leave and survive on the run.

the reason. In other places, brandishing a firearm or other weapon is permissible if it was done in the lawful defense of yourself or others. I bring all this up to point out that merely brandishing a firearm is often enough to change the thinking of individuals and groups bent on committing a crime against you. In the L.A. riots, it was enough for the Korean store owners to merely brandish their firearms (mostly) without having to fire a shot, for you see, the criminal element is far more fearful of an armed civilian than an armed cop. They know that the police go through extensive amounts of training to find creative ways to deal with their criminal activity without shooting antagonists with anything worse than pepper spray or a Taser. Just watch the episodes of *Cops* or any other reality law enforcement show. How many times do you see an officer actually fire a gun on camera? I think I've seen it exactly once, and I have watched *Cops* from its inception. I'm sure there are other times I may have missed gunplay, but the act of police officers shooting criminal suspects just doesn't happen very often, especially when you consider the number of times police are called to deal with wayward members of the public.

On the flip side, the criminal element knows that civilians have not gone through anywhere near the same amount of training that law enforcement officers do. And the majority of training participated in by civilians who can afford it deals how to shoot people *better*, not how to *avoid* shooting them. You, Mr. or Mrs. or Miss Civilian, are an unknown quantity to them. Criminals have no idea how you will react to their predations beyond that your tolerance level will likely be far lower than a cop's. You the civilian are not likely to hear the comments we hear, like, "What are ya gonna do, shoot me?" when you point a gun at them. What *you* are likely to hear are their feet moving quickly in a direction away from you.

It doesn't always go that way. Sometimes you will have to shoot a criminal bent on doing you in, or at least at them, to get their attention and turn it away from you. Just look at the compilation of accounts in the "Armed Citizen" column of the NRA's *American Rifleman* magazine, as I have since age 15 or so. At least 50 percent of the accounts, sometimes more, reveal that brandishing works much of the time—but be prepared if it doesn't. You should never point a firearm at a person hoping to just scare them off. You must be willing to pull that trigger if need be.

Perfect Practice

There are a lot of ways to train to become expert with your cache of firearms. Paper or steel target shooting at basic square ranges is better than nothing and certainly has its place in getting down the basics of marksmanship. If you can afford to take advance courses like those offered at Gunsite, Thunder Ranch, or TDI here in Ohio, take advantage of it, but don't think it is a necessity. Read materials from well-known experts such as the late Col. Jeff Cooper (I learned to shoot a handgun and shoot it well just by following the directions in one of his books from the 1970s), or others like Bill Jordan. I also commend to you the book *On Combat* by Col. David Grossman, which explains the intricacies of deadly combat and what you may experience in those situations.

Dry-fire practice and become so familiar with your weapons systems that you can operate (including field stripping) your weapons even in the dark. Dry-fire saves ammo. (Just don't do that with your rimfire guns, as there's a strong probability you'll break a firing pin).

To be most effective, your survival weapons should be of limited types. This doesn't mean that the only rifles you can have are ARs. It just means there shouldn't be a bunch of different action types involved. There's nothing wrong in my book with relying both on AKs and ARs, which would be only two weapon types to be proficient with. But start throwing in bolt guns or HK- or FN-style weapons on top of your preferred type and you're setting yourself up for human-induced malfunction. I think I'm pretty good with operating just about any type of commonly encountered action system out there for small arms, but that's under normal day-to-day conditions. It is *not* while fighting for my life under extreme stress. Ideally, I would want to work with only one type of system per weapon, be it rifle, shotgun, or handgun.

We have all heard that practice makes perfect, but I'm here to tell

Practice is essential, and the more you can get, the better off you'll be when the balloon goes up. Training on a par with what's available to S.W.A.T. teams is available to civilians. Do your research, and if you have the means to participate in this kind of advanced tactical preparation, by all means, take advantage of it.

you that is wrong. It's "perfect practice that makes perfect," which means that, if you're doing stuff wrong, you are ingraining bad habits into your patterns of behaviors and skills—and you will perform as you have trained.

When it comes to firearms training, it is not a matter of round count ("Yea, dude, I just blew up 1,000 rounds at the range today—there wasn't a beer can left in sight!"), it's the rounds that count. In other words, you're going to learn to be judicious in your training. Each round you send downrange must be effective. When the time comes, you can't afford to spray and pray to get the job done, not because of the danger to innocents per se, but because you won't be able to run to your favorite gun store the next day and get more ammo.

In addition to constantly striving to put round after round through the same hole with your survival weapons at all the distances you train, there are two other particular areas I think make good basic range training. These are weapon transition drills and magazine retention.

Addressing the first one, you need to train to switch from one weapon to another in case of a weapons failure. For instance, at CQB ranges, it may be quicker to switch from an empty or jammed AK or AR to the holstered backup pistol until you can obtain some distance from your threat and find cover to fix the problem. So, at varying distances, load and fire a few rounds from your shotgun, AR, or AK for example, (five to 10 rounds is good, avoid two-shot drills), and then sling or simply hold onto the empty or "jammed" gun with one hand, draw your pistol, and fire four controlled rounds on your target or targets from the pistol. You should learn to transition from the pistol to the long gun, as well. Vary the round counts and distances. The use of cover should be incorporated into all your training if you can.

The second area of tactical proficiency that needs to be worked on is magazine retention. Remember the Newhall, California, shootout in 1971, where four California state highway patrolmen were murdered by two armed robbers? The officers were armed with Smith & Wesson Model 19 .357 Magnum revolvers. The two bad guys had a shotgun and a Colt .45 Auto. The bad guys survived the grisly ordeal, but through their involvement in the incident and knowledge of how the officer's responded to and handled the situation, a great number of important training lessons were learned the hard way for law enforcement.

First, according to witnesses, a couple officers looked shocked and confused when they fired their handguns, looking at them as if they were broken. Why was this? The officers were firing full-power 158-grain semi-wadcutter .357 Magnum ammo for the first time. At the range, to save money and wear and tear on the officers, they had been training only with the very mild .38 Special 148-grain wadcutter bullets. That's about 1,200 fps in velocity versus 700. No one knows for sure, but it was surmised at the time that the officers may have thought their guns were going to blow up when they experienced the unaccustomed heavy recoil and muzzle flash of the .357 Magnum round. That fact altered police training to the point where Ohio law, for example, requires that law enforcement agencies must qualify with practice ammunition that approximates the power of their duty ammunition.

By the way, another possible explanation for the officers' issues with their guns is based on Col. Grossman's research into visual and audio distortion during gunfights—information unknown back then. Grossman's studies found that the officers may have thought that their guns weren't working at all. It still happens today, due to phenomena known as auditory exclusion, and it can happen no matter the caliber or load. This is also known as "tunnel hearing," akin to "tunnel vision" and can set in at times of extreme stress—in other words, the noise of the officers' own gunfire may have perceptually receded so far in to the background that the "distorted" noise could have led them to believe they had malfunctioning guns. How can you avoid this? Train, train, and train again,\ with all the right ammo, but just being aware that this can happen is at least as important. You have to know what can happen to you physically and mentally in the middle of a gun fight *before* you get in one.

The second thing learned from that shootout is that the four officers who died, who would have loaded their spare ammo out of dump pouches or belt loops back then, were found to have empty brass casings either in their pockets or in a neat little pile on the ground at their feet. This meant that they were following the ingrained range procedure of catching the empty rounds into their hands as part of the reloading procedure, and them putting the empties into the brass can at their feet in order to keep the range neat and avoid being yelled at by the rangemaster. Immediately after this was analyzed, training for law enforcement was changed, and it became universal standard procedure to let the revolver empties fall freely to the ground, collecting them only after all shooting was done.

This procedure carried over to the autoloading pistol era, except it wasn't really the same thing. Empty brass from a semi-auto is, of course, automatically ejected away from the shooter each time a shot is fired. Problem solved there, but a new one was created. Officers and civilians were being trained to let empty or partially full magazines, an operational part of the weapon, fall to the ground and become unavailable.

Did you know the first generation Glock pistols had magazines purposely designed *not* to drop clear of the weapon when the magazine release button was pushed? That was a specification of the Austrian Army, when they adopted the pistol as their standard duty weapon. They didn't want soldiers losing magazines after firing. It was the American law enforcement community that demanded drop-free magazines from Glock, so the design was changed.

Train yourselves out of the drop-free pattern whenever you shoot, be it personal practice, competition, or qualification. During current times, dropping magazines isn't a huge concern, but in the civil disorder era, when you're on the move, you can't afford to leave behind empty or partially empty magazines. So now when you train, capture every magazine—full or empty, rifle or pistol—with your weak hand, stuff it into one of the pockets on the cargo pants you're wearing, and load in a fresh one. This is why I said much earlier that, as much as I love my M1 Garand, I would likely leave it behind because it throws its empty magazines all over creation every time it's emptied. While I might be able to recover those empties, it isn't likely to happen when rounds are incoming or when it's pitch black outside. If you want that level of power, get an M1A in .308 and catch and secure the magazines each and every time that you shoot. With all your weapons, practice shooting and reloading them with one hand only. And everyone who's going to carry a gun and provide for the common defense must train with their guns—*everyone*, men, women and children. With the kids, start them out easy, okay? Teach them first the safety and joy of shooting and shooting at fun targets. Don't start out telling them they're learning to shoot so they can shoot at people. That kind of stuff will end you up in the offices of the local Children's Services agency with a follow-up appearance on the local and maybe national news. If you're carrying other weapons for defense—pepper spray, launchers, tomahawks, knives, or even bows and arrows—train with them, as well, because your CQB could turn out to be really close and uncomfortable.

Vehicle Defense

There are times when you may have to fire at attackers from inside your car. This happens on a fairly regular basis, such as when carjackers don't realize they're attempting to ply their trade in a state that now permits concealed carry. It also happens with law enforcement officers. In these situations, it usually involves officers firing handguns from within their cars, often through their own windshield at assailants approaching their position. Recently, we had an incident here in Columbus, where an officer returned fire with his Smith & Wesson Model 4506 .45 ACP pistol, firing through his windshield against a suspect armed with a semi-auto AK-47 successfully taking down his assailant (permanently).

In the immediate aftermath of civil disorder, you may find your vehicle surrounded as you attempt to escape and evade the urban

When firing from a vehicle, try and make sure the muzzle of your weapon is outside the interior of the vehicle to avoid damaging your hearing and that of other occupants. Too, keeping a long gun at least partially outside a window can make reloading faster and less awkward.

ground zero you're in. Think of the case of Reginald Denny during the Rodney King riots in L.A. If you are alone, that means you will have to use a pistol, a *large-capacity* pistol, to drive off the crowd. That's why I travel not only with my Smith & Wesson Model 642 .38 Special with 15 rounds on my person, but also with my Beretta M9A1 with a total of 45 rounds in my Maxpedition Sitka sling pack. You cannot allow yourself to be surrounded and dragged from your vehicle, or you will be done. If you have someone riding with you, they can use a long gun, one of the short, folding-stock models, to bring more firepower to bear, hopefully keeping the muzzle outside

Your vehicle can be both a weapon and a means of defense. Here the author uses his open truck door for partial cover, a smart move, as he can quickly enter the vehicle and get going. No matter how you use your vehicle, do not allow yourself to be surrounded or dragged from it.

the window to lessen the noise impact. You can use as many people as you have weapons for to provide that 360-degree defense, and that way you can concentrate on driving.

Speaking of driving, don't be afraid to use the vehicle itself as a weapon. Your Ford pickup truck can deliver far more kinetic energy against human targets than any shoulder-fired weapon. Get away from Hollywood portrayals that never show people in a vehicle plowing through a hostile crowd to escape. If that's what it takes, do it. Do not let your vehicle get surrounded.

Earlier this year, while returning home from Gatlinburg, we were

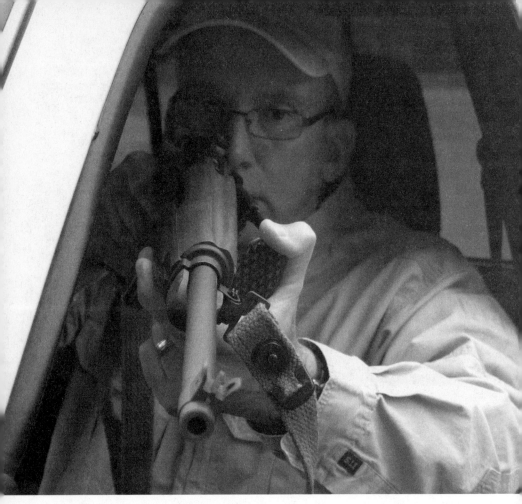

The Auto-Ordnance AOM150 Paratrooper Carbine is a great travel gun, whether you love it for its compactness with the stock folded for emergency firing from within a vehicle, for firing from outside the vehicle with the stock locked out, or for convenient and even discrete carry.

forced to drive through a less than desirable neighborhood because the freeway had been entirely shut down. It was late afternoon, and numbers of questionable people were moving about on foot in the area. There were no police cruisers available; they were all tied up due that traffic accident and were busy sealing off access at other points to the freeway. I didn't want to alarm my wife, but I withdrew the Kimber 10mm Model 1911 I was carrying in my fanny pack and slid it between my seat and the armrest without her noticing. For a period of time I drove with one hand on the wheel and one on the butt of the gun. Fortunately I didn't need to brandish this gun, although its stainless finish would have gotten any malcontent's attention, and we left the area without incident—but I made two decisions at that point. First, I need to travel with a pistol with more ammo, which is why the Beretta 92 or M9A1 is with me now. Second, my Del-Ton AR-15 was in the rear compartment of my vehicle during that trip and not within easy access. This led me to understanding the concept of a travel gun and carrying one of them in a compact case in the back seat for easy access, instead of in the trunk. I started out packing the UC9 carbine, which simplifies ammo supply, but I may switch to the Century International Folding AK or M1A1 Paratrooper Carbine. The M1A1 has better ergonomics, the AK more oomph and better ammo re-supply. We'll see. Right now, as my torn up left knee heals after surgery, the M1A1 is easier for me to handle, but either way, this should serve as a lesson in how to think through various situations and how to remain flexible as life changes.

Teaming Up

As you can see, part of the tactics of going armed for dealing with a disaster include the mindset of wanting to defend you and your family and understanding the use of firearms and other tools if you want to survive. That leads me to the concept of teaming up.

They say there's strength in numbers, and that's so simply true that such a saying almost needs no explanation. The more folks you have on your side, the better off you are—at least in most cases. But, if you're like me and don't have a large family group in the immediate area—and by immediate, I mean within a mile radius—you are

Formal training in the operational systems of each of your weapons will help you support your overall survival operation. You should know how to load, fix basic problems like a jammed magazine, and even fieldstrip your guns in the dark to say you are proficient with each weapon.

going to have to rely on not just trusted friends, but people you consider brothers and sisters. That is truly the level of trust you will need amongst each other.

The trust factor for those you team up with is of huge importance. I think there is another old adage that goes something like "If you want to know who your true friends are, go into business with them." Under high-stress situations like that, which certainly require trust, you really will find out who your friends are. Imagine what you may find out when the situation involves life or death. Throughout my career as a law enforcement officer, I've made sure to ask myself, who would I want to have "go through the door" with me in dangerous LE situations. Conversely, who as a leader would I want to follow through the very gates of Hell? I've run across a few men I'd do that for over the years, and I'm here to tell you, there aren't a whole lot of them. Concepts like that are what you will want to use to determine who is with you and who isn't. Just because a person happens to be a neighbor in the literal sense doesn't mean that they are the particular neighbor you would want to "fort up" with.

When you're making such evaluations, you must ask, what do these persons bring the table in terms of how their presence benefit you? In one of the episodes of the *Doomsday Preppers* show, there was a fellow, actually kind of a hippy that never left the '60s type of guy, who was on the right track for the most part. He had managed to purchase an abandoned nuclear missile silo site to live in and await the calamity he was expecting. He would have had a great thing going there were it not for two issues. First, the only firearm I saw that he had for defense was what appeared to be an old Mosin-Nagant bolt-action rifle hanging on a wall. When asked about the use of deadly force to protect his site, he, being truly a peace-loving hippie type, got very emotional and refused to talk about it. Clearly he wanted to rely on his isolated position, a tall chain link fence and gate, and security cameras to hold his excellent position. Kind of hard to do when people are pouring gasoline down your exterior ventilation system and lighting it to burn you out.

His other point of weakness wasn't evident until the very end of the show. The people whom he brought together to fort up with were also a group of hippies without any useful skills, other than the abilities of a couple of the freeloaders (yes, that's what I called them), whose claim to fame were that they were some sort of "spiritual advisors" to the group. These spiritual advisors would, in case of extreme calamity, lead the others in yoga and meditation exercises.

Folks, you can't eat yoga, you can't use it to repair equipment or grow food, and it is certainly not capable of repelling an assault on your facility. That is certainly why I would want my in-laws with us (familial aspects aside). My father-in-law is one of the most mechanically handy guys I know, on par with or better than my own late father. So, too, is my brother-in-law. My mother-in-law has expertise in areas of cooking and food preparation and is very expert in maintaining a household, as is my sister-in-law. I, on the other hand, stink in all those areas—but I'm pretty handy with firearms.

My Columbus Police survival expert, "Bill," has some of the same ideas in mind. Although he has a home setup (when I saw it, I thought I had entered a combined grocery store, ammo dump, and gun/gunsmith shop), that one could live off for an extended period of time, and I mean for many months, he, like me, also stinks in the area of non-firearm mechanical know-how. If a disaster event involved localized issues, he would probably stay put. If it looked like a situation involving extensive, long-term societal collapse, he'd evacuate with his kids and as much gear as he can carry in his truck to fort up with a friend who is mechanically handy and also has a self-sustaining farm equipped with a hand-pumped well for a long-term water supply. Bill already has a number of his guns located at that site and he is never without heavy firepower to extricate himself from dangerous situations while away from home.

Give careful thought to whom you bring into your anticipated situations. If you have the safe base that folks are coming to, then you are in charge. People who will not accept this fact should not be invited in. Sadly, there will be people whom you will have to turn away, especially if they know about your preparations. There was an excellent episode in the original *Twilight Zone* about this. A group of friends was having dinner together at the home of another whom they'd made fun of because he'd built a nuclear bomb shelter in his basement (in those days, that was the preeminent threat that people lived with). In the show, a nuclear attack is launched. Everyone went to their homes to await the arrival of Soviet bombers and missiles, but only for a while. They then drifted back over to ask, then demand, admittance to their former friend's bomb shelter, a place that provided only enough room for the owner, his wife, and his son.

Eventually all the neighbors ended up there, and they broke down the door to the bomb shelter. In the story, the shelter owner did not have a gun. Right after mob rule took over, the radio announced that the threat was over and the nuclear attack had been averted. The group of friends had to deal with each other and themselves in the aftermath. Not pretty at all, but a very realistic look at what one could expect to happen in our world, the world outside the *Twilight Zone*.

My friend "Bill" was very concerned about my revealing information on him and his survival setup. As you can see, I have kept his identity and location anonymous. His caution is important. When you are "Bill," you cannot brag to friends that you have no intention of supporting them or bringing them aboard with you in the event of a collapse. Your survival preparations are strictly on a need to know basis—and the people outside your trusted circle don't need to find out about it from you or the people you are teaming up with.

Field Movements & Patrol Formations

I won't pretend to be an expert in field movements and military formations, because I never served in the military. But I can tell you about some basics for small group movements based upon formations we use for active shooter intervention or S.W.A.T.-type entries and area searches.

(Left) Children in their early teens are more than capable of learning to handle the AR-15 weapon system and others. Above, a woman armed with a high-capacity Glock pistol. Forget thinking that youths and women are easily intimidated—no assailant wants to run into either of these when they're armed and confidently aiming.

There is one basic concept and one concept alone when it comes to moving afoot to get to a safer location, and that is 360-degree coverage (which, by the way, also includes up). Beyond that, foremost you will need a person to "take point," the lead. This point person is usually the most trusted person, the best fighter and shot, the one with the most experience, the person whose job it is to keep the rest of the patrol or group out of danger. They will be placed slightly ahead of your group, but not so far as to be out of contact. The individuals in your group will be assigned their own areas of responsibilities and they have to stick with them or the unity and functionality of the group will be lost.

That imperative of controlling and sticking with your area of responsibility is one of the hardest things I've found to impart to new officers during basic training or to officers undergoing S.W.A.T.-related training. It is natural human instinct, at least for those who are good cops or soldiers, to want a piece of the action, to get involved and assist. But unless the situation is dire to the extreme—as in part of the group is down—you have to let the other members of the group handle their own. Resisting that urge to overtake and assume the responsibilities of others requires discipline and practice.

Training of your group in anticipation of a calamity should be accomplished as much as possible without making it obvious to the casual observer what you are training for, or that you are even training at all. Group movement, for example, can be practiced, unarmed or at least lightly armed, without calling attention to your activities. Think of going through your practice scenarios as if you were simply taking a nature hike. It will be somewhat harder to do this in densely populated areas without calling attention to yourselves, but it is possible to do. In addition to your point person, you will need coverage at the following points based on a clock face, if you have enough armed personnel. The point will be at 12 o'clock, with other personnel covering at the two, four, six, eight, and 10 o'clock positions. In the center of the protection will be the people who cannot provide well for their own defense, the aged or infirm, young children, and anyone else who needs assistance.

Do not rely on a GPS when you travel through locations unfamiliar to you. None of us know how bad things will be, but you should consider that the satellite system that relays the information to your GPS may not work anymore. Furthermore, it is possible that, depending on what the situation is, civilian access to the signals could be limited. So a compass and good regional maps that include topography will be essential. Don't know how to use one? One of my Army Special Forces friends, who had been an Eagle Scout, recommends the *Boy Scout Handbook* or *Orienteering* Merit Badge book to the soldiers he trains as being one of the best laid out and easiest way to comprehend map reading with a compass.

An example of partial concealment, with the defender using the outstanding 6.8 SPCII Wilson Combat Recon AR and a 2.5x10 Nightforce illuminated reticle scope. The camo pattern on the defender's clothing is the now passé Army digital.

Cover/Concealment/Body Armor

It's important to understand the concepts of cover and concealment, as well as how body armor might play into your plans. Let's start with the basics and assume that you are entirely new to this topic.

On its face, cover versus concealment isn't difficult to understand. Cover is a barrier that tends to stop incoming bullets and helps hide your position. Cover can be earthen banks, trees, vehicles, buildings, etc. Concealment, on the other hand only hides your *position*. Think tall grass, for instance. Concealment is selected when cover is not available—cover is *always* your first choice. Simple, right?

Hold it a minute, cover is only cover based upon what kinds of rounds are coming your direction. For example, a motor vehicle, such as the police cruisers involved in the great L.A. bank robbery of 1997, were Ford Crown Victorias or former Chevy Impalas (the real ones built body on frame with 350 CI V-8 engines). These work great as cover when the rounds being fired at you are defensive-type pistol rounds like 9mm, .40, or .45—*not* rounds like the .500 Smith & Wesson—and most shotgun rounds. However, the officers in that 1997 situation were being shot at with weapons firing full metal jacket 7.62x39mm rounds traveling about 2300 fps. Those rounds *tore up* the cars that were in direct, straight-line proximity to the robbers.

Dirt and trees are usually good cover, but if someone is shooting a .338 Lapua or .50 BMG at your position, then all bets are off. I instruct my police cadets that cover is usually a fleeting thing. It may be effective for a while, but it can be eaten away by the right round fired against it.

During some of my casual testing many years ago, I decided to test the power of .38 Special versus .357 Magnum 158-grain lead semi-wadcutter bullets fired against cinder blocks (I used four-inch-barreled revolvers in the test). Cinder block walls are fairly good cover, in many cases. In my test, the .38 Special bullets fired against these blocks made a .35-inch diameter chip or dent in the block and precious little else. When I loaded the same gun (I believe it was a Ruger Security Six) with the .357 Magnum rounds, the block *crumbled* with the first shot. A single-row wall being pounded with this round would soon have holes punched through it with this weapon, and I daresay that rounds like the .41 and .44 Magnum and bigger would be even more destructive. The lesson here is don't assume you're safe behind cinder block or any other cover when your assailant "only" has a handgun. It all depends on the caliber and what particular round and load is in it.

I have mixed feelings about body armor for my personal calamity survival plan. I have worn soft body armor religiously since it became available to me in 1984. I don't recall a time of not wearing it when on any form of duty. It is a critical piece of police gear, and anyone who won't wear it on duty is a fool.

But, and this is a big but, the soft body armor I wear beneath my uniform shirt is rated to stop only the most commonly encountered pistol calibers. It will not stop rifle fire unless there's an armored plate in the armor's carrier designed for such things. This is why the armor-piercing (AP) version of the 5.7x28mm isn't available to civilians. It will still punch through soft body armor when fired not only out of the PS90 carbine, but also out of the Five-seveN pistol.

When I wear my body armor, I'm traveling about in my police cruiser with access to air conditioning for most of my shift. I'm not walking with it on for miles. It takes NIJ (National Institutes of Justice) Level IV heavy-duty S.W.A.T. armor with armor plates to stop AP rounds. How many realize how heavy this type of armor is? The answer is, not many of you. I have worn that armor only for short-term purposes, such as on S.W.A.T. raids, where I was

A poured concrete basement foundation wall should provide reasonably good cover against all but the heaviest and most powerful incoming rounds.

driven to the site in a van and had a distance of less than 100 yards to traverse by foot, including all the distances covered in whatever structure we were in. I would never wear that level of protection on an open area rural search unless I was searching for someone known to be armed with a rifle. It is so heavy it makes you clumsy, and that is one of the primary reasons cops don't wear this much protection all the time.

Good armor is expensive, especially the stuff that stops rifle fire (and which is not normally available to civilians), and it is hot and heavy. If any Kevlar-type soft armor is worn constantly and gets sweaty, gets wet too often from rainfall, or is much older than five years, it is on its way to failure. If I felt the need for armor, I would get NIJ Level II concealable armor and perhaps add an armor plate, a small one, for the center of the chest (assuming there's a pocket for one).

Since, armor has more limitations than you may have thought, I think there are better ways to spend your resources. For instance, used armor could be purchased and placed in the door panels of your car or rolled up in your windows to protect the glass (and you) from blunt-force trauma coming your way.

Protection By Your Vehicle

When cover versus concealment was discussed earlier, I mentioned automobiles as cover. Cars and trucks make the best cover when they are moving, as it's much harder to hit a moving target in an area that disables the engine or the driver. The thing to remember here is that, if you are trying to clear out of a contested area in your car, keep low and keep driving. Only try to shoot if your vehicle is being overrun, otherwise focus on your driving. You are likely to make it out against all but the most withering fire from high-powered rifles.

Pistol bullets are small and low powered. They will rapidly disable an auto only with a lucky shot. The most vulnerable area in any car is the side window safety glass, which is designed to break easily to allow access to or egress from a vehicle in an emergency. Windshield and rear window glass is laminated glass. A thin sheet of clear plastic binds two sections of glass together in the middle. It is much harder for bullets to penetrate laminated glass, especially if the vehicle is moving and particularly if the window has a significant sloping angle to it, such as on a sports car.

Shooting tires does *not* rapidly disable a vehicle and certainly doesn't make a vehicle blow up and flip over. Tires also don't pop when hit by bullets. They're made of synthetic rubber and steel and Kevlar

Survival situations will require teamwork with family and friends. Everyone in your group should be trained, and communication between team members will be paramount to surviving whatever disaster you're involved in. Who's shooting and when? Who's moving and who's staying put? Your success as a team will depend on this kind of coordination and more.

fiber—just the kind of stuff you make body armor out of. You can drive a long way even on tires that have been totally destroyed by police spike strips. Just watch the evening news or episodes of *Cops*. Watch the vehicles continue to drive for a long distance (albeit much slower), on the steel rims only, as they throw up a rooster tail shower of sparks.

One last thought on this subject. A basic principle of carrying a gun either off-duty as a cop or with a license as a concealed carry permit holder is that the presence of that gun or guns does not make you invincible. If it did, we would never have cops killed or injured from anything other than automobile-related events. When I'm off-duty, I don't want confrontation. Just because I have a firearm(s), doesn't mean that I can or should drive through any neighborhood with impunity. If dangerous areas can be avoided, then do so. The route around them may be longer, but the issue for us is not one of the shortest distance between points, but, rather, what is the safest. Where can I drive without fear of being swarmed or carjacked, or even struck by unintended gunfire? No matter how many guns and guys/gals you have with you, always take the path of least resistance.

Indirect Ricochet Fire

In order to perform in a superior manner with a firearm, you have to understand not only its and your limitations, but also things it can do that may be advantageous to your situation. One of those advantageous characteristics of a rifle, shotgun, or pistol to be familiar with is the possibility of directing effective indirect or ricochet fire against a partially obscured opponent, who may be prone on the ground. Projectiles fired at less than a 45-degree angle to a hard surface (concrete, asphalt, hard packed earth, water, and brick or cinder block walls), don't act like pool balls and just and bounce away at the same angle they came in. They bounce up and travel parallel with that hard surface, six to eight inches above it, until they impact something in their path. Yes, the bullet or shot may be deformed, but it's gonna hurt what it hits, like a bad guy's head—or your head while you hide under a car. The principle works both ways; it's a law of physics. Understanding this phenomena means you can use it to your advantage in a firefight, knowing that your aim doesn't always need to be direct or even in line of sight to be effective. Which brings me to the next area of concern, suppressive fire.

Suppressive Fire

Suppressive fire means exactly what it says. You are using your outgoing rounds to suppress, control, or stop the opponent's incoming rounds. Generally, this means that, in order to actually cause a suppressive affect, your rounds need to be more accurate than your opponent's or greater in number than your opponent can produce.

One event that showed the use of fire suppression against an enemy happened in the Trolley Stop Mall, in Utah. An off-duty cop was eating lunch in the food court with his wife, when a nutcase began opening fire on innocent patrons. The officer got his wife down and then went after the shooter with his Kimber .45. But because he'd listened to the wrong person about gun advice—his bud told him that the magazine springs needed to "rest" on occasion— he had downloaded to six rounds in each, rather than the eight he could have carried. He also had just one spare magazine. Yet, by judicious, accurate fire, he was able to suppress the shooter, keeping him pinned in a hallway until the uniformed boys came in to assist. The off-duty guy was on his last one or two rounds when the troops arrived. I don't think he hit the gunman, as he didn't have a direct shot, but he didn't need to. The rounds from his gun had the bad guy pinned down, his position suppressed.

As was said, in most of the post-calamity situations we'll be in, especially when away from home, we'll need to conserve ammo. Therefore, most of our fire suppression should be based on accurate, rather than voluminous, fire.

Beating Back the Mob—Riot Guns

The traditional riot gun, the 12-gauge pump shotgun, can still be effectively deployed against a crowd. While it is certainly lethal, it can also be deployed in a potentially less-lethal manner, simply by using the bouncing bullet technique, which means those 00 Buckshot pellets will strike with less velocity after being shot at an angle against the ground in front of the mob. The pellets will strike the shins and feet of the rioters, and while the wounds from lead pellets will be more severe than wounds from bouncing rubber or wooden pellets, unless the person on the receiving end is unlucky, should not prove to be fatal (at least not immediately). A few rounds should turn a crowd.

I would only use this technique against a crowd not visibly armed with firearms and far enough away that deploying the shotgun thusly is not unsafe. However, if that doesn't appear to be working, you need to be selective in your target, and not for reasons of fear of collateral damage, but rather what should be a fear of being overrun, having a limited supply of ammo, and perhaps facing superior forces. There is only one answer to this problem besides retreat—which would be the best choice—and that is taking out those who appear to be the leaders.

While there is such a thing as mob mentality, which allows people to act as a collective body that's free of individual responsibility, there are certain people who are the encouragers of such action, the leaders, and they need to be taken out and taken out fast. Several years ago, there were major problems in Columbus with unruly students and interlopers rioting on or near the Ohio State Campus following the outcome of OSU Buckeye football games. Officers tried to deal with this, but were ineffective at first. After a number of these incidents, CPD started becoming more selective in what they were doing, interspersing undercover officers amid the crowd to identify the instigators. As soon as that was done, those people were taken out and arrested, nearly immediately. By doing that, the police took a lot of wind out of the sails of those who were present. Other monitoring actions followed, and there hasn't been rioting on campus in several years now.

Chapter 12

EMERGENCY EVACUATION: NEEDS BEYOND THE GUN

F ood, water, and medical considerations are of the second biggest level of importance compared to the selection of firearms, and one could argue easily that they're the first, but having all the food you need is of no value if you can't defend and keep it. One of the things I noticed on the *Doomsday Preppers* television series was that a few folks had stockpiled a huge amount of stored food, but were planning on an emergency evacuation anyway and, thus, would leave the majority of their food stocks behind, since they didn't have enough vehicles or large enough vehicles to carry it all.

There may be occasions when there simply isn't enough time to load everything, even if your vehicle situation would allow for it. If you have the money to spare to buy a bunch of stuff and then lose it when you abandon it, then good for you. I don't have that luxury, so I believe that, to prepare properly

This is one of survival expert "Bill's" ammo supplies. Yes, I wish I had that much too. But if there is a big chance you will be evacuating rather than staying when the crisis hits, can you take all this with you? Not likely, unless you are not planning on eating, drinking, or changing clothes. If you are staying in a fixed, fortified location, this is great. If there is a better than 50/50 chance you are leaving, it is likely too much. It would be good to have the capability of burying in safe storage any excess—no big deal if the lawless get some leftover food, but it's certainly a problem if they get your leftover guns and ammo.

for all scenarios, whether you may or may not have to abandon your home, then you need to find a balance. You have to take enough to keep you going for an extended period if you leave and have enough to get you by if you stay. If you have a place that is absolutely defensible, such as the abandoned U.S. missile silo a group of folks I know collectively owns, then stockpile away. If you don't and if you know that you absolutely *will* leave when disaster strikes, then only store up food supplies that can go with you.

One of the very best systems for out there for emergency evacuation food supplies comes from a company called Food Insurance (www.foodinsurance.com.) I obtained a sample of its Essentials two-week kit. Contained in a quality backpack designed for long-term carry, the Essentials kit contains enough food for three meals a day for one person for two weeks, or two persons for one week. This is not only an ideal kit to store at home in preparation for evacuation, but also to take with you when taking trips out of town by car for business or pleasure. The meals are freeze-dried, which allows them to be stored for the very long term (seven to 10 years), while maintaining good taste if properly prepared. Like the late Karl Malden said in the American Express ads of old, "Don't leave home without it."

For $199.99, the Essentials Kit contains the following two-week, three-meal-a-day food supply, all sealed in a Mylar bag. Examples of the meals contained in the bag are granola, oatmeal, or a protein shake for breakfast, and lasagne, beef stroganoff, or creamy chicken rotini for lunch/dinner. Extras include supplies of rice and powdered electrolyte drinks, matches, a cooking tin, and a reusable heat source. There's also a water filter with a capacity for 1,500-plus uses that will filter a total of a 100 gallons of water, safeguarding you against nasty bacteria that can make you very sick or kill you.

Keep in mind that clean drinking water will be your primary concern in terms of physical well being, as you can die of dehydration within 10 days or so, while true starvation will take four to six weeks, depending on your physical build and condition. Again, while this could seem to be your absolute priority, in the end it won't matter how much water or food you have if you can't keep it.

I like the Food Insurance kit—*a lot*. It doesn't contain anything nonessential, gimmicky, or cheap, like some competing systems do. I particularly like the water purification system. With this, you

A town in the Midwest after a devastating tornado. Some have lost all, some not much, but it's almost a sure thing that the entire community is without the essentials of food, fuel, water, and power. Are you prepared to face this if your house is still standing? Are you prepared to face it if it's not? You have to think through all the scenarios to be fully prepared.

don't have to carry loads of water with you, something that will weigh you down—*big time*. A small, on-hand amount of sealed bottled water will suffice unless you're traveling through desert area in the American Southwest, where an empty purifying bottle isn't going to be of much help. For that situation, you'll have to load up on the bottled water and use the purification system as backup.

For $50 you can upgrade and get the Emergency Plus Kit. This adds a small first aid kit, multi-tool, and hand crank radio/ flashlight combo. I have not been able to check into the quality of these upgrade items. From the photos the multi-tool appears to

Properly canned food can last years and a supply like this is a great one to have if you're sheltering in place. But no one in their right mind would want to backpack glass jars if they have to evacuate. For surviving on the run, think Army MREs and other more portable food sources that can be prepared with little more than water and some sort of heat source.

When stocking up on food, water, and first-aid/medical supplies, remember your pets. This is especially true if you have service animals, such as the author's wife's seeing eye guide dog.

be Leatherman in style, but the brand is unknown. Knowing the company's other kits, I'd guess that the quality of these extra items is adequate, but I wouldn't say this about kits that claim to cover every aspect of survival situations. So, while I have no fear that the Food Insurance tool is of acceptable quality, I'd rather pick out my own tool, such as a Gerber Multi-plier, than blindly order one as part of a kit.

Multi-use electronic items are another "survival kit" feature you'll find out there. However, you can't rely on all of them to meet all your needs. For instance, in my somewhat younger and more naïve days, I purchased a multi-use electronic survival radio. It seemed like a good idea at the time. It had an AM/FM radio, an eight-inch screen black-and-white TV set (that was before broadcast signals were changed from analogue to digital, so that equipment would be of no use now), and a removable, incandescent (that's all that was available then) flashlight. I didn't really purchase this gadget for true "survival needs," I purchased it to keep from going stir crazy after the great ice storm of 2004, when our power was out. The unit was only about $60 at the time.

Don't waste your money on stuff like this. If you want a good radio, buy a good radio. I have a 15-year-old Radio Shack battery-operated AM/FM shortwave radio that my wife and I got a lot of use from during this summer's major storm-induced power outage. It really kept us up to date on the situation. Radio Shack still has a large selection of this type of radio available, including hand crank models. In any event, don't rely on one piece of equipment to serve all your needs. Obviously, if you already have all the components you need for your food-related survival kit, e.g. lights, first aid kits, and multiple use tools, then I would bypass the upgraded kit.

One last thought about food and water, and that is you'll need to

A first-aid kit is a must, whether you're staying or going, and it should include more than a seven-day cache of prescription meds. Too, everyone in your survival convoy should have a grasp on the basics of CPR, tourniquet use, making a splint or neck brace, and other emergency medical aid. Training for such things can usually be found through the Red Cross and other like-minded organizations.

remember that your pets or service animals need those, too. We have a total of three dogs, two are pets that also serve as our intruder detection system and the third is my wife's seeing eye guide dog. Since most people will want to take their companion animals with them in the case of an evacuation, we need to provide for them, both out of love and necessity. The only pet food that is easily stored is canned dog food, so my wife and I started stockpiling that. It should last for a long time under the right conditions, plus it can always be rotated out. You may also want to have flea and tick treatments on hand.

Flashlights, batteries, candles, matches, radios, food, and water are all essential items to have ready and close at hand when facing an emergency situation. Keep a supply in your home, your car, your office, and your luggage when you travel (if possible). You never know when disaster will strike, but you will be prepared to face it when it does.

Medicine and Other Supplies

As one gets older, one relies on more and more medications in order to keep the body functioning at levels that would have been unheard of just 50 years ago. When I engage in vacation or business travel these days, I never carry just a seven-day pill-minder-type supply. I take the entire bottle so that, in the event I'm delayed, I will have the meds I need close at hand for up to two weeks. That's prepared, but I also know that, when the crisis occurs, I'll need much more than that.

If you can't get large enough prescription fill amounts locally from your doctor or insurance, there are other avenues available online. I am not recommending that you do this, as it's possible the medications you are ordering may not contain what is advertised, I am simply saying it is an option to be explored. Some unused prescriptions may be beneficial to hold onto for potential later use, such as narcotic pain pills. I would hate to be caught without them in case of a kidney stone or some other such unpleasantness.

Clothing and Sanitation

These things are bigger issues than you might think. You're going to need clothing that is durable, but also that will assist you in packing along the supplies that you need, This means you should have on hand cargo-type shirts and pants, especially the pants. The 5.11 brand makes some of the best and its garments are commonly used by cops. They hold up quite well, and the basic pant has spare pistol mag pockets on both sides in addition to the cargo pockets; you can use those for cell phones right now, but perhaps not in the future. In any event, you won't want to carry everything you need in a pack. You need pocket support.

One other clothing issue to think about. What time of year is it now or will it be soon? The German Army made this lack of forethought a decided mistake in WWII, as they advanced into the Soviet Union without the benefit of winter clothing. Yea, it was nice when they started, and because of their arrogance and overconfidence they expected to conquer all the Soviet Union before winter set in. Were they ever wrong. Think ahead a little.

Sanitation is an even bigger issue. I experienced the lack of flush toilets for five days, the longest period yet, when the big storm of 2012 came through and we lost power, which included power to our well. I had prepared for such an eventuality by stockpiling 30 or so gallons of water. I got darned tired after awhile of filling up the toilet tank for each flush. My wife, city girl that she is and even though she is an experienced camper, really didn't like being Amish for five days (and no disrespect there, we have considerable admiration for their hardiness). In the aftermath of the storms, we purchased a generator for the next round.

One of the things a generator can't make, however, is toilet paper. The Sears catalog was, at one time, popular for use in outhouses, but I don't want to use it now, even if there was still such a thing. Time to stock up on TP for the future, as it's a *very* valuable commodity.

Still, there are worse issues. If there is a disruption of water and sewer service in the cities or suburbs, then diseases like cholera once again begin to raise their ugly and deadly heads. Dysentery, too, will become commonplace, because living situation in many place will suddenly drop to third-world standards. Handwashing with anti-bacterial soaps will become crucial and ensuring the safety of your water and food supply will become paramount. The Soviet Army lost their war in large part, a *very* large part, in Afghanistan, because their soldiers were never taught that it was a good idea to wash ones hands after defecation. They lost more troops to dysentery and related conditions than they did to enemy bullets.

In any event, the collapse will not be a pretty sight for anyone, even for the most prepared. But those people, people such as my friend "Bill," people who may have been looked askance at by others, will be the only people living in anything near what we once called comfort. Bring on the ridicule, but don't come running to me for help once it happens. As I recall from the Bible, Noah was ridiculed by people who later ended up waterlogged, so you and those who believe in what we're doing are in the best of company.

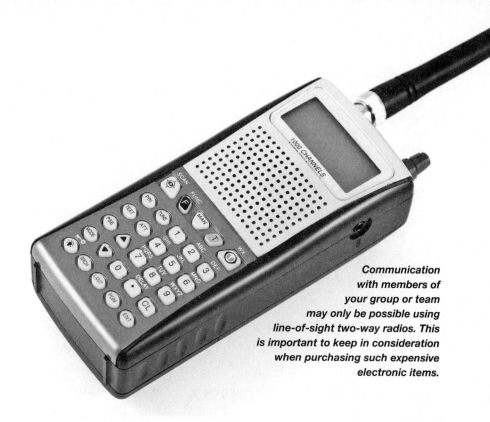

Communication with members of your group or team may only be possible using line-of-sight two-way radios. This is important to keep in consideration when purchasing such expensive electronic items.

Communication

Depending on how bad things get and what the cause is for the condition, it's likely cell phone communications and the Internet will be gone for an extended period of time. If the chaos is due to a 1929-style economic collapse, there will be no cell phone communication, simply because of the number of people trying to access it, just like on 9/11. In the longer term, things will cascade down. Landlines may be available for a while, but there's no telling how long. Shortwave radio communications may also be a possibility, but it's most likely that primary communication is going to be mouth to mouth and direct contact and observation.

No matter how sophisticated we seem to get, the first casualty of a widespread natural or man-made disaster is the loss of all communications. It is the major chink in the armor of public safety forces every-where, unless they have a quantity of extremely expensive satellite radios that will work in any situation short of a missile attack on satellites.

If you have access to some line-of-site radios for your group, they could mean the difference between life and death. Marine band or commercial radios will give you the longest range without the public being able to listen in like they would if your radio system was a CB radio. Motorola multi-band commercial radios can be had for $250 to $500 a pop. They are more expensive, but are of better quality than any handheld CB radio you can buy.

This is the type of radio that public safety forces in the Katrina aftermath relied on. Their daily use repeater system, that is the system of towers that provides signal boost to handheld and vehicle-mounted radios giving them extended range (this is a really basic explanation), was knocked out. Thus, the only communication these public safety people had to use with each other (and it took awhile to get these op-eration), was a limited number of commercial line-of-sight radios.

Recovery

Aftermath recovery is hard to predict, because we've been discuss-ing armed preparation for a very wide variety of potentialities local-ized, statewide, multi-state, national, and even international in scope. Obviously, recovery depends on the severity of the incident/s. The thought of the United States of America suddenly finding itself in the status of a third-world country has been beyond the realm of thought throughout the majority of time our country has existed—but that's not the case any longer. We are pushing closer to that status with the passing of every day it seems. If there is not a change of attitude and fortunes soon, I fear we will end up there. If not, and I hope it's not,

There are a hundred toilet paper jokes out there, but none of them are funny if you run out of this very serious commodity. You probably haven't thought about it yet, but you absolutely need to have this on your stockpiling list.

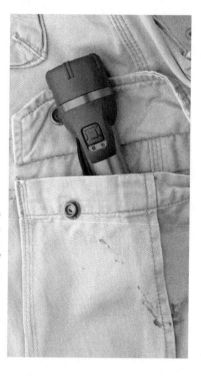

Of course you're going to pack clothing, but it better be functional. Cargo pants keep things like flashlights and knives close at hand where they're needed most and free up your pack for other items.

then I'll get to do what I truly want to do, and that is reach a healthy retirement age and relax. But if it is going to come down, I want to be as ready for it as possible. I want to be able to protect my wife and family and my trusted friends if I can until things can return to a better state of normal—and I hope we never have to endure that wait.

Silver, Not Gold

Here's a little bit of advice that I picked up from the novel *Patriots, a Novel of Survival in the Coming Collapse,* by James Wesley Rawles. If you have never read this book, I highly recommend you do, for there are a lot of good ideas contained therein.

If times come to what many people are expecting, a total societal collapse, the only things that will be worth money are the tangibles. Your stock portfolio and retirement fund will be out the window, at least for a while and maybe permanently. This means guns, ammo, food, and cash in the form of solid gold or silver (i.e., not paper).

For several years now, the gold market has shown explosive growth, with prices going from $300 or so an ounce at the start of the Obama administration to nearly $1,700 now. Pure silver is sitting around $28 per ounce. The point that was made in Rawles' book is that you won't be able to buy much gold to barter with at current prices and you will certainly *not* get an equal amount of goods in return for what you paid for the gold. Silver, on the other hand is a much better choice for barter, as you can receive fairer value.

Instead of trying to save up for a few pieces of gold, I have been purchasing silver rounds in half- and one-ounce sizes from APMEX (American Precious Metals Exchange, Inc.). The company offers a variety of forms the gold and silver can take, and in that includes old coins for their silver content. I say this, because paying for silver coins that have an added value for rarity beyond the actual silver content doesn't make sense

and it won't count for anything more in collapse conditions. Do what you want, but I would purchase silver in the form of rounds (and not just for collapse, but to supplement your retirement portfolio). Make sure you are buying actual *physical* gold or silver, not some sort of promissory note, and keep what you purchase in that fireproof Liberty safe you took home for your guns.

The Shape of Things

Speaking of your physical condition, what kind of shape are you in? One episode of *Doomsday Preppers* featured a gentleman who had all the right ideas and, as I recall, a pretty good level of preparedness, but who must have weighed in at 300 or more pounds. To me he was reaching the point of morbid obesity.

Only the strong survive, folks, and you need some level of fitness and well being to compete. I recently turned 55. I led police recruits in extensive physical fitness testing for 25 years at my law enforcement agencies and our training academies,

Only the strong survive. If you're serious about making it through a societal collapse or extended natural disaster, it will pay to be in the best physical shape you can before such calamity strikes.

and today my knees and feet can't take the pounding of running any more. However, I haven't stopped training, and today I make good use of stationary bicycles at the local YMCA. We older folks are going to have to compete with a much younger crowd of amoral or immoral aggressors in the event of civil breakdown. While we have a wealth of experience on our side that will allow us to prevail, we won't succeed if we have let ourselves deteriorate. It's up to you. How serious are you about surviving?

BE INFORMED, BE PREPARED, BE READY
TO SURVIVE

STAY ALIVE Whatever emergency comes your way you can be prepared to survive and thrive by covering the basics. You'll learn survival kit essentials, building shelter, purifying water, and successfully navigating any environment, from this top-selling survival guide.

LIVING READY MAGAZINE With an avalanche of survival & preparedness information rolling your way at nearly every turn, it can be a little tough figuring out what to trust, which tactics to take, and the preparations that will help you get out alive. That's why the team at *Gun Digest* teamed with survival experts to bring you *Living Ready Magazine*.

Check out more in the Survival section of GunDigest.com

WHAT'S IN YOUR BUG-OUT BAG? *Gun Digest the Magazine* asked, and real people like you answered with their "recipes" for their perfect survival kits. In this single reference you'll glean valuable bug-out bag advice from 15 of those very prepared people about first aid tips, shelter options, navigation techniques, food and water preparations, and protection gear to help you get through any disaster.